PENGUIN BOOKS — GREAT IDEAS

Revolution and War

Karl Marx
1818–1883

Karl Marx

Revolution and War

PENGUIN BOOKS — GREAT IDEAS

PENGUIN BOOKS

Published by the Penguin Group
Penguin Books Ltd, 80 Strand, London wc2r orl, England
Penguin Group (USA) Inc., 375 Hudson Street, New York, New York 10014, USA
Penguin Group (Canada), 90 Eglinton Avenue East, Suite 700, Toronto, Ontario,
Canada m4p 2y3 (a division of Pearson Penguin Canada Inc.)
Penguin Ireland, 25 St Stephen's Green, Dublin 2, Ireland (a division of Penguin Books Ltd)
Penguin Group (Australia), 250 Camberwell Road, Camberwell, Victoria 3124, Australia
(a division of Pearson Australia Group Pty Ltd)
Penguin Books India Pvt Ltd, 11 Community Centre, Panchsheel Park, New Delhi – 110 017, India
Penguin Group (NZ), 67 Apollo Drive, Rosedale, North Shore 0632, New Zealand
(a division of Pearson New Zealand Ltd)
Penguin Books (South Africa) (Pty) Ltd, 24 Sturdee Avenue, Rosebank, Johannesburg 2196, South Africa

Penguin Books Ltd, Registered Offices: 80 Strand, London wc2r orl, England

www.penguin.com

All pieces were first published in *The New York Tribune* on the individual dates shown below:
'Revolution in China and in Europe' first published June 14, 1853
'The British Rule in India' first published June 25, 1853
'Chartism' first published July 14, 1853
'The Greek Insurrection' first published March 29, 1854
'The English Middle Class' first published August 1, 1854
'Declaration of War – On the History of the Eastern Question' first published April 15, 1854
'Revolution in Spain – Bomarsund' first published September 4, 1854
'Prussia' first published May 5, 1856
'Revolution in Spain [I]' first published August 8, 1856
'Revolution in Spain [II]' first published August 18, 1856
'On Italian Unity' first published January 24, 1859
'The North American Civil War' first published October 25, 1861
'The News and Its Effect in London' first published December 19, 1861
'Progress of Feeling in England' first published December 25, 1861
'English Public Opinion' first published February 1, 1862
This selection first published in Penguin Books 2009

1

Set by Rowland Phototypesetting Ltd, Bury St Edmunds, Suffolk
Printed in England by Clays Ltd, St Ives plc

ISBN: 978-0-141-39932-4

www.greenpenguin.co.uk

Penguin Books is committed to a sustainable future
for our business, our readers and our planet.
The book in your hands is made from paper
certified by the Forest Stewardship Council.

Contents

Revolution in China and in Europe

1859

A most profound yet fantastic speculator on the principles which govern the movements of Humanity, was wont to extol as one of the ruling secrets of nature, what he called the law of the contact of extremes. The homely proverb that 'extremes meet' was, in his view, a grand and potent truth in every sphere of life; an axiom with which the philosopher could as little dispense as the astronomer with the laws of Kepler or the great discovery of Newton.

Whether the 'contact of extremes' be such a universal principle or not, a striking illustration of it may be seen in the effect the Chinese revolution seems likely to exercise upon the civilized world. It may seem a very strange, and a very paradoxical assertion that the next uprising of the people of Europe, and their next movement for republican freedom and economy of government, may depend more probably on what is now passing in the Celestial Empire, – the very opposite of Europe, – than on any other political cause that now exists, – more even than on the menaces of Russia and the consequent likelihood of a general European war. But yet it is no paradox, as all may understand by attentively considering the circumstances of the case.

Whatever be the social causes, and whatever religious,

dynastic, or national shape they may assume, that have brought about the chronic rebellions subsisting in China for about ten years past, and now gathered together in one formidable revolution, the occasion of this outbreak has unquestionably been afforded by the English cannon forcing upon China that soporific drug called opium. Before the British arms the authority of the Manchu dynasty fell to pieces; the superstitious faith in the eternity of the Celestial Empire broke down; the barbarous and hermetic isolation from the civilized world was infringed; and an opening was made for that intercourse which has since proceeded so rapidly under the golden attractions of California and Australia. At the same time the silver coin of the Empire, its lifeblood, began to be drained away to the British East Indies.

Up to 1830, the balance of trade being continually in favor of the Chinese, there existed an uninterrupted importation of silver from India, Britain and the United States into China. Since 1833, and especially since 1840, the export of silver from China to India has become almost exhausting for the Celestial Empire. Hence the strong decrees of the Emperor against the opium trade, responded to by still stronger resistance to his measures. Besides this immediate economical consequence, the bribery connected with opium smuggling has entirely demoralized the Chinese State officers in the Southern provinces. Just as the Emperor was wont to be considered the father of all China, so his officers were looked upon as sustaining the paternal relation to their respective districts. But this patriarchal authority, the only moral link embracing the vast machinery of the State, has gradually been corroded by the corruption of those officers, who have made great gains by conniving at opium smuggling. This has occurred principally in the same Southern provinces where the rebellion commenced. It is almost needless to observe that, in the same measure in which opium has obtained the sovereignty over the Chinese, the Emperor and his staff of pedantic mandarins have become dispossessed of their own sovereignty. It would seem as though history had first to make this whole people drunk before it could rouse them out of their hereditary stupidity.

Though scarcely existing in former times, the import of English cottons, and to a small extent of English woollens, has rapidly risen since 1833, the epoch when the monopoly of trade with China was transferred from the East India Company to private commerce, and on a much greater scale since 1840, the epoch when other nations, and especially our own, also obtained a share in the Chinese trade. This introduction of foreign manufactures has had a similar effect on the native industry to that which it formerly had on Asia Minor, Persia and India. In China the spinners and weavers have suffered greatly under this foreign competition, and the community has become unsettled in proportion.

The tribute to be paid to England after the unfortunate war of 1840, the great unproductive consumption of opium, the drain of the precious metals by this trade, the destructive influence of foreign competition on native manufactures, the demoralized condition of the public administration, produced two things: the old taxation became more burdensome and harassing, and new taxation was added to the old. Thus in a decree of the Emperor, dated Peking, Jan. 5, 1853, we find orders given to the viceroys and governors of the southern provinces of Wu-chang and Hang-Yang to remit and defer the payment of taxes, and especially not in any case to exact more than the regular amount; for otherwise, says the decree, 'how will the poor people be able to bear it?' 'And thus, perhaps,' continues the Emperor, 'will my people, in a period of general hardship and distress be exempted from the evils of being pursued and worried by the tax-gatherer.'

Such language as this, and such concessions we remember to have heard from Austria, the China of Germany, in 1848.

All these dissolving agencies acting together on the finances, the morals, the industry, and political structure of China, received their full development under the English cannon in 1840, which broke down the authority of the Emperor, and forced the Celestial Empire into contact with the terrestrial world. Complete isolation was the prime condition of the preservation of Old China. That isolation having come to a violent end by the medium of England, dissolution must follow as surely as that of any mummy carefully preserved in a hermetically sealed coffin, whenever it is brought into contact with the open air. Now, England having brought about the revolution of China, the question is how that revolution, will in time react on England, and through England on Europe. This question is not difficult of solution.

The attention of our readers has often been called to the unparalleled growth of British manufactures since

1850. Amid the most surprising prosperity, it has not been difficult to point out the clear symptoms of an approaching industrial crisis. Notwithstanding California and Australia, notwithstanding the immense and unprecedented emigration, there must ever without any particular accident, in due time arrive a moment when the extension of the markets is unable to keep pace with the extension of British manufactures, and this disproportion must bring about a new crisis with the same certainty as it has done in the past. But, if one of the great markets suddenly becomes contracted, the arrival of the crisis is necessarily accelerated thereby. Now, the Chinese rebellion must, for the time being, have precisely this effect upon England. The necessity for opening new markets, or for extending the old ones, was one of the principal causes of the reduction of the British tea-duties, as, with an increased importation of tea, an increased exportation of manufactures to China was expected to take place. Now, the value of the annual exports from the United Kingdom to China amounted, before the repeal in 1833 of the trading monopoly possessed by the East India Company, to only £600,000; in 1836, it reached the sum of £1,326,388; in 1845, it had risen to £2,394,827; in 1852, it amounted to about £3,000,000. The quantity of tea imported from China did not exceed, in 1793, 16,167,331 lbs.; but in 1845, it amounted to 50,714,657 lbs.; in 1846, to 57,584,561 lbs.; it is now above 60,000,000 lbs.

The tea crop of the last season will not prove short, as shown already by the export lists from Shanghai, of 2,000,000 lbs. above the preceding year. This excess is to be accounted for by two circumstances. On one hand, the state of the market at the close of 1851 was much depressed, and the large surplus stock left has been thrown into the export of 1852. On the other hand, the recent accounts of the altered British legislation with regard to imports of tea, reaching China, have brought forward all the available teas to a ready market, at greatly enhanced prices. But with respect to the coming crop, the case stands very differently. This is shown by the following extracts from the correspondence of a large tea-firm in London:

In Shanghai the terror is extreme. Gold has advanced upward of 25 per cent., *being eagerly sought for hoarding*, silver has so far disappeared that *none could be obtained* to pay the China dues on the British vessels requiring port clearance; and in consequence of which Mr Alcock has consented to become responsible to the Chinese authorities for the payment of these dues, on receipt of East India Company's bills, or other approved securities. *The scarcity of the precious metals* is one of the most unfavorable features, when viewed in reference to the immediate future of commerce, as this abstraction occurs precisely at that period when their use is most needed, to enable the tea and silk buyers to go into the interior and effect their purchases, for which a *large portion of bullion is paid in advance, to enable the producers to carry on their operations* . . . At this period of the year it is usual to begin making arrangements for the new teas, whereas at present nothing is talked of but the means of protecting person and property, all transactions being at a stand . . . If the means are not applied to secure the leaves in April and May, the early crop, which includes all the finer descriptions, both of black and green teas, will be as much lost as unreaped wheat at Christmas.

Now the means for securing the tea leaves, will certainly not be given by the English, American or French squadrons stationed in the Chinese seas, but these may easily, by their interference, produce such complications, as to cut off all transactions between the tea-producing interior and the tea-exporting sea ports. Thus, for the present crop, a rise in the prices must be expected – speculation has already commenced in London – and for the crop to come a large deficit is as good as certain. Nor is this all. The Chinese, ready though they may be, as are all people in periods of revolutionary convulsion, to sell off to the foreigner all the bulky commodities they have on hand, will, as the Orientals are used to do in the apprehension of great changes, set to hoarding, not taking much in return for their tea and silk, except hard money. England has accordingly to expect a rise in the price of one of her chief articles of consumption, a drain of bullion, and a great contraction of an important market for her cotton and woolen goods. Even *The Economist*, that optimist conjuror of all things menacing the tranquil minds of the mercantile community, is compelled to use language like this: 'We must not flatter ourselves with finding as extensive a market for our exports to China [. . .] It is more probable that our export trade to China should suffer, and that there should be a diminished demand for the produce of Manchester and Glasgow.'

It must not be forgotten that the rise in the price of

so indispensable an article as tea, and the contraction of so important a market as China, will coincide with a deficient harvest in Western Europe, and, therefore, with rising prices of meat, corn, and all other agricultural produce. Hence contracted markets for manufactures, because every rise in the prices of the first necessaries of life is counterbalanced, at home and abroad, by a corresponding deduction in the demand for manufactures. From every part of Great Britain complaints have been received on the backward state of most of the crops. *The Economist* says on this subject:

In the South of England not only will there be left much land unsown, until too late for a crop of any sort, but much of the sown land will prove to be foul, or otherwise in a bad state for corn-growing. On the wet or poor soils destined for wheat, signs that mischief is going on are apparent. The time for planting mangel-wurzel may now be said to have passed away, and very little has been planted, while the time for preparing land for the turnip is rapidly going by, without any adequate preparation for this important crop having been accomplished . . . Oat-sowing has been much interfered with by the snow and rain. Few oats were sown early, and late sown oats seldom produce a large crop . . . In many districts losses among the breeding flocks have been considerable.

The price of other farm-produce than corn is from 20 to 30, and even 50 per cent. higher than last year. On the Continent, corn has risen comparatively more than in England. Rye has risen in Belgium and Holland full 100 per cent. Wheat and other grains are following suit.

Under these circumstances, as the greater part of the regular commercial circle has already been run through by British trade, it may safely be augured that the Chinese revolution will throw the spark into the overloaded mine of the present industrial system and cause the explosion of the long-prepared general crisis, which, spreading abroad, will be closely followed by political revolutions on the Continent. It would be a curious spectacle, that of China sending disorder into the Western World while the Western powers, by English, French and American war-steamers, are conveying 'order' to Shanghai, Nanking, and the mouths of the Great Canal. Do these order-mongering powers, which would attempt to support the wavering Manchu dynasty, forget that the hatred against foreigners and their exclusion from the Empire, once the mere result of China's geographical and ethnographical situation, have become a political system only since the conquest of the country by the race of the Manchu Tartars? There can be no doubt that the turbulent dissensions among the European nations who, at the later end of the 17th century, rivaled each other in the trade with China, lent a mighty aid to the exclusive policy adopted by the Manchus. But more than this was done by the fear of the new dynasty, lest the foreigners might favor the discontent existing among a large proportion of the Chinese during the first half century or thereabouts of their subjection to the Tartars. From these considerations, foreigners were then prohibited from all communication with the Chinese, except through Canton, a town at a great distance from Peking and the tea-districts, and their commerce restricted to intercourse with the Hong merchants, licensed by the Government expressly for the foreign trade, in order to keep the rest of its subjects from all connection with the odious strangers. In any case an interference on the part of the Western Governments at this time can only serve to render the revolution more violent, and protract the stagnation of trade.

At the same time it is to be observed with regard to India, that the British Government of that country depends for full one seventh of its revenue on the sale of opium to the Chinese, while a considerable proportion of the Indian demand for British manufactures depends on the production of that opium in India. The Chinese, it is true, are no more likely to renounce the use of opium than are the Germans to forswear tobacco. But as the new Emperor is understood to be favorable to the culture of the poppy and the preparation of opium in China itself, it is evident that a death-blow is very likely to be struck at once at the business of opium-raising in India, the Indian revenue, and the commercial resources of Hindostan. Though this blow would not immediately be felt by the interests concerned, it would operate effectually in due time, and would come in to intensify and prolong the universal financial crisis whose horoscope we have cast above.

Since the commencement of the eighteenth century there has been no serious revolution in Europe which had not been preceded by a commercial and financial crisis. This applies no less to the revolution of 1789 than to that of 1848. It is true, not only that we every day behold more threatening symptoms of conflict between the ruling powers and their subjects, between the State and society, between the various classes; but also the conflict of the existing powers among each other gradually reaching that height where the sword must be drawn, and the *ultima ratio* of princes be recurred to. In the European capitals, every day brings dispatches big with universal war, vanishing under the dispatches of the following day, bearing the assurance of peace for a week or so. We may be sure, nevertheless, that to whatever height the conflict between the European powers may rise, however threatening the aspect of the diplomatic horizon may appear, whatever movements may be attempted by some enthusiastic fraction in this or that country, the rage of princes and the fury of the people are alike enervated by the breath of prosperity. Neither wars nor revolutions are likely to put Europe by the ears, unless in consequence of a general commercial and industrial crisis, the signal of which has, as usual, to be given by England, the representative of European industry in the market of the world.

It is unnecessary to dwell on the political consequences such a crisis must produce in these times, with the unprecedented extension of factories in England, with the utter dissolution of her official parties, with the whole State machinery of France transformed into one immense swindling and stock-jobbing concern, with Austria on the eve of bankruptcy, with wrongs everywhere accumulated to be revenged by the people, with the conflicting interests of the reactionary powers themselves, and with the Russian dream of conquest once more revealed to the world.

The British Rule in India

[. . .] Last night the debate on India was continued in the House of Commons, in the usual dull manner. Mr Blackett charged the statements of Sir Charles Wood and Sir J. Hogg with bearing the stamp of optimist falsehood. A lot of Ministerial and Directorial advocates rebuked the charge as well as they could, and the inevitable Mr Hume summed up by calling on Ministers to withdraw their bill. Debate adjourned.

Hindostan is an Italy of Asiatic dimensions, the Himalayas for the Alps, the Plains of Bengal for the Plains of Lombardy, the Deccan for the Apennines, and the Isle of Ceylon for the Island of Sicily. The same rich variety in the products of the soil, and the same dismemberment in the political configuration. Just as Italy has, from time to time, been compressed by the conqueror's sword into different national masses, so do we find Hindostan, when not under the pressure of the Mohammedan, or the Mogul, or the Briton, dissolved into as many independent and conflicting States as it numbered towns, or even villages. Yet, in a social point of view, Hindostan is not the Italy, but the Ireland of the East. And this strange combination of Italy and of Ireland, of a world of voluptuousness and of a world of woes, is anticipated in the ancient traditions of the religion of Hindostan. That religion is at once a religion of sensualist exuberance, and a religion of self-torturing asceticism; a religion of the Lingam and of the Juggernaut; the religion of the Monk, and of the Bayadere.

I share not the opinion of those who believe in a golden age of Hindostan, without recurring, however, like Sir Charles Wood for the confirmation of my view, to the authority of Khuli-Khan. But take, for example, the times of Aurangzeb; or the epoch, when the Mogul appeared in the North, and the Portuguese in the South; or the age of Mohammedan invasion, and of the Heptarchy in Southern India; or, if you will, go still more back to antiquity, take the mythological chronology of the Brahman himself, who places the commencement of Indian misery in an epoch even more remote than the Christian creation of the world.

There cannot, however, remain any doubt but that the misery inflicted by the British on Hindostan is of an essentially different and infinitely more intensive kind than all Hindostan had to suffer before. I do not allude to European despotism, planted upon Asiatic despotism, by the British East India Company, forming a more monstrous combination than any of the divine monsters startling us in the Temple of Salsette. This is no distinctive feature of British Colonial rule, but only an imitation of the Dutch, and so much so that in order to characterize the working of the British East India Company, it is sufficient to literally repeat what Sir Stamford Raffles, the *English* Governor of Java, said of the old Dutch East India Company:

The Dutch Company, actuated solely by the spirit of gain, and viewing their [Javan] subjects, with less regard or consideration than a West India planter formerly viewed a gang upon his estate, because the latter had paid the purchase money of human property, which the other had not, employed all the existing machinery of despotism to squeeze from the people their utmost mite of contribution, the last dregs of their labor, and thus aggravated the evils of a capricious and semi-barbarous Government, by working it with all the practised ingenuity of politicians, and all the monopolizing selfishness of traders.

All the civil wars, invasions, revolutions, conquests, famines, strangely complex, rapid, and destructive as the successive action in Hindostan may appear, did not go deeper than its surface. England has broken down the entire framework of Indian society, without any symptoms of reconstitution yet appearing. This loss of his old world, with no gain of a new one, imparts a particular kind of melancholy to the present misery of the Hindoo, and separates Hindostan, ruled by Britain, from all its ancient traditions, and from the whole of its past history.

There have been in Asia, generally, from immemorial times, but three departments of Government; that of Finance, or the plunder of the interior; that of War, or the plunder of the exterior; and, finally, the department of Public Works. Climate and territorial conditions, especially the vast tracts of desert, extending from the Sahara, through Arabia, Persia, India, and Tartary, to the most elevated Asiatic highlands, constituted artificial irrigation by canals and water-works the basis of Oriental agriculture. As in Egypt and India, inundations are used for fertilizing the soil in Mesopotamia, Persia, &c.; advantage is taken of a high level for feeding irrigative canals. This prime necessity of an economical and common use of water, which, in the Occident, drove private enterprise to voluntary association, as in Flanders and Italy, necessitated, in the Orient, where civilization was too low and the territorial extent too vast to call into life voluntary association, the interference of the centralizing power of Government. Hence an economical function devolved upon all Asiatic Governments, the function of providing public works. This artificial fertilization of the soil, dependent on a Central Government, and immediately decaying with the neglect of irrigation and drainage, explains the otherwise strange fact that we now find whole territories barren and desert that were once brilliantly cultivated, as Palmyra, Petra, the ruins in Yemen, and large provinces of Egypt, Persia, and Hindostan; it also explains how a single war of devastation has been able to depopulate a country for centuries, and to strip it of all its civilization.

Now, the British in East India accepted from their predecessors the department of finance and of war, but they have neglected entirely that of public works. Hence the deterioration of an agriculture which is not capable of being conducted on the British principle of free competition, of *laissez-faire* and *laissez-aller*. But in Asiatic empires we are quite accustomed to see agriculture deteriorating under one government and reviving again under some other government. There the harvests correspond to good or bad government, as they change in

Europe with good or bad seasons. Thus the oppression and neglect of agriculture, bad as it is, could not be looked upon as the final blow dealt to Indian society by the British intruder, had it not been attended by a circumstance of quite different importance, a novelty in the annals of the whole Asiatic world. However changing the political aspect of India's past must appear, its social condition has remained unaltered since its remotest antiquity, until the first decennium of the 19th century. The hand-loom and the spinning-wheel, producing their regular myriads of spinners and weavers, were the pivots of the structure of that society. From immemorial times, Europe received the admirable textures of Indian labor, sending in return for them her precious metals, and furnishing thereby his material to the goldsmith, that indispensable member of Indian society, whose love of finery is so great that even the lowest class, those who go about nearly naked, have commonly a pair of golden ear-rings and a gold ornament of some kind hung round their necks. Rings on the fingers and toes have also been common. Women as well as children frequently wore massive bracelets and anklets of gold or silver, and statuettes of divinities in gold and silver were met with in the households. It was the British intruder who broke up the Indian hand-loom and destroyed the spinning-wheel. England began with driving the Indian cottons from the European market; it then introduced twist into Hindostan, and in the end inundated the very mother country of cotton with cottons. From 1818 to 1836 the export of twist from Great Britain to India rose in the proportion of 1 to 5,200. In 1824 the export of British muslins to India hardly amounted to 1,000,000 yards, while in 1837 it surpassed 64,000,000 of yards. But at the same time the population of Dacca decreased from 150,000 inhabitants to 20,000. This decline of Indian towns celebrated for their fabrics was by no means the worst consequence. British steam and science uprooted, over the whole surface of Hindostan, the union between agriculture and manufacturing industry.

These two circumstances – the Hindoo, on the one hand, leaving, like all Oriental peoples, to the Central Government the care of the great public works, the prime condition of his agriculture and commerce, dispersed, on the other hand, over the surface of the country, and agglomerated in small centers by the domestic union of agricultural and manufacturing pursuits – these two circumstances had brought about since the remotest times, a social system of particular features – the so-called *village system*, which gave to each of these small unions their independent organization and distinct life. The peculiar character of this system may be judged from the following description, contained in an old official report of the British House of Commons on Indian affairs:

A village, geographically considered, is a tract of country comprising some hundred or thousand acres of arable and waste lands; politically viewed it resembles a corporation or township. Its proper establishment of officers and servants consists of the following descriptions: The *potail*, or head inhabitant, who has generally the superintendence of the affairs of the village, settles the disputes of the inhabitants, attends to the police, and performs the duty of collecting the revenue within his village, a duty which his personal influence and minute acquaintance with the situation and concerns of the people render him the best qualified for this charge. The *kurnum* keeps the accounts of cultivation, and registers everything connected with it. The *tallier* and the *totie*, the duty of the former of which consists . . . in gaining information of crimes and offenses, and in escorting and protecting persons traveling from one village to another; the province of the latter appearing to be more immediately confined to the village, consisting, among other duties, in guarding the crops and assisting in measuring them. The *boundary-man*, who preserves the limits of the village, or gives evidence respecting them in cases of dispute. The Superintendent of Tanks and Watercourses distributes the water . . . for the purposes of agriculture. The Brahmin, who performs the village worship. The schoolmaster, who is seen teaching the children in a village to read and write in the sand. The calendar-brahmin, or astrologer, &c. These officers and servants generally constitute the establishment of a village; but in some parts of the country it is of less extent, some of the duties and functions above described being united in the same person; in others it exceeds the above-named number of individuals . . . Under this simple form of municipal government, the inhabitants of the country have lived from time immemorial. The boundaries of the villages . . . have been but seldom altered; and though the villages themselves have been sometimes injured, and even desolated by war, famine or disease, the same name, the same limits, the same interests, and even the same families have continued for ages. The inhabitants gave themselves no trouble about the breaking up and divisions of kingdoms;

while the village remains entire, they care not to what power it is transferred, or to what sovereign it devolves; its internal economy remains unchanged. The *potail* is still the head inhabitant, and still acts as the petty judge or magistrate, and collector or renter of the village.

These small stereotype forms of social organism have been to the greater part dissolved, and are disappearing, not so much through the brutal interference of the British tax-gatherer and the British soldier, as to the working of English steam and English free trade. Those family-communities were based on domestic industry, in that peculiar combination of hand-weaving, hand-spinning and hand-tilling agriculture which gave them self-supporting power. English interference having placed the spinner in Lancashire and the weaver in Bengal, or sweeping away both Hindoo spinner and weaver, dissolved these small semi-barbarian, semi-civilized communities, by blowing up their economical basis, and thus produced the greatest, and to speak the truth, the only *social* revolution ever heard of in Asia.

Now, sickening as it must be to human feeling to witness those myriads of industrious patriarchal and inoffensive social organizations disorganized and dissolved into their units, thrown into a sea of woes, and their individual members losing at the same time their ancient form of civilization, and their hereditary means of subsistence, we must not forget that these idyllic village communities, inoffensive though they may appear, had always been the solid foundation of Oriental despotism, that they restrained the human mind within the smallest possible compass, making it the unresisting tool of superstition, enslaving it beneath traditional rules, depriving it of all grandeur and historical energies. We must not forget the barbarian egotism which, concentrating on some miserable patch of land, had quietly witnessed the ruin of empires, the perpetration of unspeakable cruelties, the massacre of the population of large towns, with no other consideration bestowed upon them than on natural events, itself the helpless prey of any aggressor who deigned to notice it at all. We must not forget that this undignified, stagnatory, and vegetative life, that this passive sort of existence evoked on the other part, in contradistinction, wild, aimless, unbounded forces of destruction and rendered murder itself a religious rite in Hindostan. We must not forget that these little communities were contaminated by distinctions of caste and by slavery, that they subjugated man to external circumstances instead of elevating man the sovereign of circumstances, that they transformed a self-developing social state into never changing natural destiny, and thus brought about a brutalizing worship of nature, exhibiting its degradation in the fact that man, the sovereign of nature, fell down on his knees in adoration of Kanuman, the monkey, and Sabbala, the cow.

England, it is true, in causing a social revolution in Hindostan, was actuated only by the vilest interests, and was stupid in her manner of enforcing them. But that is not the question. The question is, can mankind fulfil its destiny without a fundamental revolution in the social state of Asia? If not, whatever may have been the crimes of England she was the unconscious tool of history in bringing about that revolution.

Then, whatever bitterness the spectacle of the crumbling of an ancient world may have for our personal feelings, we have the right, in point of history, to exclaim with Goethe:

> Sollte diese Qual uns quälen
> Da sie unsre Lust vermehrt,
> Hat nicht myriaden Seelen
> Timur's Herrschaft aufgezehrt?

['Should this torture then torment us / Since it brings us greater pleasure? / Were not through the rule of Timur / Souls devoured without measure?']

Chartism

1859

[. . .] Strikes and combinations of workmen are proceeding rapidly, and to an unprecedented extent. I have now before me reports on the strikes of the factory hands of all descriptions at Stockport, of smiths, spinners, weavers, etc., at Manchester, of carpet-weavers at Kidderminster, of colliers at the Ringwood Collieries, near Bristol, of weavers and loomers at Blackburn, of loomers at Darwen, of the cabinet-makers at Boston, of the bleachers, finishers, dyers and power-loom weavers of Bolton and neighborhood, of the weavers of Barnsley, of the Spitalfields broad-silk weavers, of the lace makers of Nottingham, of all descriptions of workingmen throughout the Birmingham district, and in various other localities. Each mail brings new reports of strikes; the turn-out grows epidemic. Every one of the larger strikes, like those at Stockport, Liverpool, etc., necessarily generates a whole series of minor strikes, through great numbers of people being unable to carry out their resistance to the masters, unless they appeal to the support of their fellow-workmen in the Kingdom, and the latter, in order to assist them, asking in their turn for higher wages. Besides it becomes alike a point of honor and of interest for each locality not to isolate the efforts of their fellow-workmen by submitting to worse terms, and thus strikes in one locality are echoed by strikes in the remotest other localities. In some instances the demands for higher wages are only a settlement of long-standing arrears with the masters. So with the great Stockport strike.

In January, 1848, the mill-owners of the town made a general reduction of 10 per cent. from all descriptions of factory-workers' wages. This reduction was submitted to upon the condition that when trade revived the 10 per cent. was to be restored. Accordingly the work-people memorialized their employers, early in March, 1853, for the promised advance of 10 per cent.; and as they would not come to arrangements with them, upward of 30,000 hands struck. In the majority of instances, the factory-workmen affirmed distinctly their *right* to *share* in the prosperity of the country, and especially in the prosperity of their employers.

The distinctive feature of the present strikes is this, that they began in the lower ranks of unskilled labor (not factory labor), actually trained by the direct influence of emigration, according to various strata of artizans, till they reached at last the factory people of the great industrial centers of Great Britain; while at all former periods strikes originated regularly from the heads of the factory-workers, mechanics, spinners, &c., spreading thence to the lower classes of this great industrial hive, and reaching only in the last instance, to the artizans. This phenomenon is to be ascribed solely to emigration.

There exists a class of philanthropists, and even of socialists, who consider strikes as very mischievous to the interests of the 'workingman himself,' and whose great aim consists in finding out a method of securing permanent average wages. Besides, the fact of the industrial cyclus, with its various phases, putting every such average wages out of the question. I am, on the very contrary, convinced that the alternative rise and fall of wages, and the continual conflicts between masters and men resulting therefrom, are, in the present organization of industry, the indispensable means of holding up the spirit of the laboring classes, of combining them into one great association against the encroachments of the ruling class, and of preventing them from becoming apathetic, thoughtless, more or less well-fed instruments of production. In a state of society founded upon the antagonism of classes, if we want to prevent Slavery in fact as well as in name, we must accept war. In order to rightly appreciate the value of strikes and combinations, we must not allow ourselves to be blinded by the apparent insignificance of their economical results, but hold, above all things, in view their moral and political consequences. Without the great alternative phases of dullness, prosperity, over-excitement, crisis and distress, which modern industry traverses in periodically recurring cycles, with the up and down of wages resulting from them, as with the constant warfare between masters and men closely corresponding with those variations in wages and profits, the working-classes of Great Britain, and of all Europe, would be a heart-broken, a weak-minded, a worn-out, unresisting mass, whose self-emancipation would prove as impossible as that of the slaves of Ancient Greece and Rome. We must not forget that strikes and combinations among the serfs were the hot-beds of the mediaeval communes, and that those communes have been in their turn, the source of life of the now ruling bourgeoisie [. . .]

The Greek Insurrection

1854

The insurrection among the Greek subjects of the Sultan, which caused such alarm at Paris and London, has now been suppressed, but its revival is thought not impossible. With regard to this possibility we are able to say that after a careful investigation of the documents relating to the whole affair so far, we are convinced that the insurgents were found exclusively among the mountaineers inhabiting the southern slope of the Pindus, and that they met with no sympathy on the part of the other Christian races of Turkey, save the pious freebooters of Montenegro; and that the occupants of the plains of Thessaly, who form the only compact Greek community still living under Turkish supremacy, are more afraid of their compatriots than of the Turks themselves. It is not to be forgotten that this spiritless and cowardly body of population did not dare to rise even at the time of the Greek war of independence. As to the remainder of the Greek race, numbering perhaps 300,000 souls, distributed throughout the cities of the Empire, they are so thoroughly detested by the other Christian tribes that, whenever a popular movement has been successful, as in Servia and Wallachia, it has resulted in driving away all the priests of Greek origin, and in supplying their places by native pastors.

But although the present Greek insurrection, considered with reference to its own merits, is altogether insignificant, it still derives importance from the occasion it affords to the western Powers for interfering between the Porte and the great majority of its subjects in Europe, among whom the Greeks count only one million against ten millions of the other races professing the Greek religion. The Greek inhabitants of the so-called kingdom as well as those living in the Ionian Isles under British rule consider it, of course, to be their national mission to expel the Turks from wherever the Greek language is spoken, and to annex Thessaly and Epirus to a State of their own. They may even dream of a Byzantine restoration, although, on the whole, they are too astute a people to believe in such a fancy. But these plans of national aggrandizement and independence on the part of the Greeks; proclaimed at this moment in consequence of Russian intrigues, as is proved by the lately detected conspiracy of the priest Athanasius, and proclaimed too by the robbers of the mountains without being reechoed by the agricultural population of the plain – all have nothing to do with the religious rights of the subjects of Turkey with which an attempt is made to mix them up.

As we learn from the English journals and from notice given in the House of Lords by Lord Shaftesbury, and in the Commons by Mr Monckton Milnes, the British Government is to be called upon in connection, partly at least, with these Greek movements to take measures to meliorate the condition of the Christian subjects of the Porte. Indeed, we are told explicitly that the great end aimed at by the western Powers is to put the Christian religion on a footing of equal rights with the Mahometan in Turkey. Now, either this means nothing at all, or it means the granting political and civil rights, both to Mussulmans and Christians, without any reference to either religion, and without considering religion at all. In other words, it means the complete separation of State and Church, of Religion and Politics. But the Turkish State, like all Oriental States, is founded upon the most intimate connection, we might almost say, the identity of State and Church, of Politics and Religion. The Koran is the double source of faith and law, for that Empire and its rulers. But how is it possible to equalize the faithful and the Giaour, the Mussulman and the Rajah before the Koran? To do that it is necessary, in fact, to supplant the Koran by a new civil code, in other words to break down the framework of Turkish society and create a new order of things out of its ruins.

On the other hand, the main feature that distinguishes the Greek confession from all other branches of the Christian faith, is the same identification of State and Church, of civil and ecclesiastical life. So intimately inter-woven were State and Church in the Byzantine Empire, that it is impossible to write the history of the one without writing the history of the other. In Russia the same identity prevails, although there, in contradistinc-tion to the Byzantine Empire, the Church has been transformed into the mere tool of the State, the instru-ment of subjugation at home and of aggression abroad. In the Ottoman Empire in conformity with the Oriental notions of the Turks, the Byzantine theocracy has been allowed to develop itself to such a degree, that the parson of a parish is at the same time the judge, the mayor, the teacher, the executor of testaments, the assessor of taxes, the ubiquitous factotum of civil life, not the servant, but the master of all work. The main reproach to be cast upon the Turks in this regard is not that they have crippled the privileges of the Christian priesthood, but, on the contrary, that under their rule this all-embracing oppressive tutelage, control, and interference of the Church has been permitted to absorb the whole sphere of social existence. Mr Fallmerayer very amusingly tells us, in his *Orientalische Briefe*, how a Greek priest was quite astonished when he informed him that the Latin clergy enjoyed no civil authority at all, and had to perform no profane business. 'How,' exclaimed the priest, 'do our Latin brethren contrive to kill time?'

It is plain then that to introduce a new civil code in Turkey, a code altogether abstracted from religion, and based on a complete separation of State and Church, would be not only to abolish Mahometanism, but also to break down the Greek Church as now established in that Empire. Can any one be credulous enough to believe in good earnest that the timid and reactionary valetudinarians of the present British Government have ever conceived the idea of undertaking such a gigantic task, involving a perfect social revolution, in a country like Turkey? The notion is absurd. They can only entertain it for the purpose of throwing dust in the eyes of the English people and of Europe.

The English Middle Class

1854

And as regards the journeyman of all descriptions, in what relation does he stand to his employer? All know with what opposition the employers met the 'Ten Hours' bill. The Tories, out of spite for the recent loss of the Corn Laws, helped the working class to get it; but when passed, the reports of the district supervisors show with what shameless cunning and petty under-hand treacheries it was evaded. Every subsequent attempt in Parliament to subject Labor to more humane conditions has been met by the middle-class representatives with the catch-cry of Communism! Mr Cobden has acted thus a score of times. Within the workshops for years the aim of the employers has been to prolong the hours of labor beyond human endurance, and by an unprincipled use of the contract system, by pitting one man against another, to cut down the earning of the skilled to that of the unskilled laborer. It was this system that at last drove the Amalgamated Engineers to revolt, and the brutality of the expressions that passed current among the masters at that time showed how little of refined or humane feeling was to be looked for from them. Their boorish ignorance was further displayed in the employment by the Masters' Association of a certain third-rate litterateur, Sidney Smith, to undertake their defense in the public press and to carry on the war of words with their revolted hands. The style of their hired writer well fitted the task he had to perform, and when the battle was over, the Masters, having no more need of literature or the press, gave their hireling his congé. Although the middle class do not aim at the learning of the old school, they do not for that cultivate either modern science or literature. The ledger, the desk, business, that is education sufficient. Their daughters, when expensively educated, are superficially endowed with a few 'accomplishments;' but the real education of the mind and the storing it with knowledge is not even dreamed of.

The present splendid brotherhood of fiction-writers in England, whose graphic and eloquent pages have issued to the world more political and social truths than have been uttered by all the professional politicians, publicists and moralists put together, have described every section of the middle class from the 'highly genteel' annuitant and Fundholder who looks upon all sorts of business as vulgar, to the little shopkeeper and lawyer's clerk. And how have Dickens and Thackeray, Miss Brontë and Mrs Gaskell painted them? As full of presumption, affectation, petty tyranny and ignorance; and the civilized world has confirmed their verdict with the damning epigram that it has fixed to this class that 'they are servile to those above, and tyrannical to those beneath them.'

The cramped and narrow sphere in which they move is to a certain degree due to the social system of which they form a part. As the Russian nobility live uneasily betwixt the oppression of the Czar above them and the dread of the enslaved masses below them, so the English middle class are hemmed in by the aristocracy on the one hand and the working classes on the other. Since the peace of 1815, whenever the middle class have wished to take action against the aristocracy, they have told the working classes that their grievances were attributable to some aristocratic privilege and monopoly. By this means the middle class roused the working classes to help them in 1832 when they wanted the Reform Bill, and, having got a Reform Bill *for themselves*, have ever since refused one to the working classes – nay, in 1848, actually stood arrayed against them armed with special constable staves. Next, it was the repeal of the Corn Laws that would be the panacea for the working classes. Well, this was won from the aristocracy, but the 'good time' was not yet come, and last year, as if to take away the last possibility of a similar policy for the future, the aristocracy were compelled to accede to a tax on the succession to real estate – a tax which the same aristocracy had selfishly exempted themselves from in 1793, while they imposed it on the succession to personal estate. With this rag of a grievance vanished the last chance of gulling the working classes into the belief that their hard lot was due solely to aristocratic legislation. The eyes of the working classes are now fully opened: they begin to cry: 'Our St Petersburg is at Preston!' Indeed, the last eight months have seen a strange spectacle in the town – a standing army of 14,000 men and women sub-sidized by the trades unions and workshops of all parts of the United Kingdom, to fight out a grand social battle for mastery with the capitalists, and the capitalists of Preston, on their side, held up by the capitalists of Lancashire.

Whatever other shapes this social struggle may hereafter assume, we have seen only the beginning of it. It seems destined to nationalize itself and present phases never before seen in history; for it must be borne in mind that though temporary defeat may await the working classes, great social and economical laws are in operation which must eventually insure their triumph. The same industrial wave which has borne the middle class up against the aristocracy, is now assisted as it is and will be by emigration bearing the working classes up against the middle classes. Just as the middle class inflict blows upon the aristocracy, so will they receive them from the working classes. It is the instinctive perception of this fact that already fetters the action of that class against the aristocracy. The recent political agitations of the working classes have taught the middle class to hate and fear overt political movements. In their cant, 'respectable men don't join them, Sir'. The higher middle classes ape the aristocracy in their modes of life, and endeavor to connect themselves with it. The consequence is that the feudalism of England will not perish beneath the scarcely perceptible dissolving processes of the middle class; the honor of such a victory is reserved for the working classes. When the time shall be ripe for their recognized entry upon the stage of political action, there will be within the lists three powerful classes confronting each other – the first representing the land; the second, money; the third, labor. And as the second is triumphing over the first, so, in its turn, it must yield before its successor in the field of political and social conflict.

Declaration of War – On the History of the Eastern Question

1854

War has at length been declared. The Royal Message was read yesterday in both Houses of Parliament; by Lord Aberdeen in the Lords, and by Lord J. Russell in the Commons. It describes the measures about to be taken as 'active steps to oppose the encroachments of Russia upon Turkey.' To-morrow *The London Gazette* will publish the official notification of war, and on Friday the address in reply to the message will become the subject of the Parliamentary debates.

Simultaneously with the English declaration, Louis Napoleon has communicated a similar message to his Senate and *Corps Législatif*.

The declaration of war against Russia could no longer be delayed, after Captain Blackwood, the bearer of the Anglo-French *ultimatissimum* to the Czar, had returned, on Saturday last, with the answer that Russia would give to that paper no answer at all. The mission of Capt. Blackwood, however, has not been altogether a gratuitous one. It has afforded to Russia the month of March, that most dangerous epoch of the year, to Russian arms.

The publication of the secret correspondence between the Czar and the English Government, instead of provoking a burst of public indignation against the latter, has – *incredibile dictu* – been the signal for the press, both weekly and daily, for congratulating England on the possession of so truly national a Ministry. I understand, however, that a meeting will be called together for the purpose of opening the eyes of a blinded British public on the real conduct of the Government. It is to be held on Thursday next in the Music Hall, Store-st.; and Lord Ponsonby, Mr Layard, Mr Urquhart, etc., are expected to take part in the proceedings.

The *Hamburger Correspondent* has the following: 'According to advices from St Petersburg, which arrived here on the 16th inst., the Russian Government proposes to publish various other documents on the Eastern question. Among the documents destined for publication are some letters written by Prince Albert.'

It is a curious fact that the same evening on which the Royal Message was delivered in the Commons, the Government suffered their first *defeat* in the present session; the second reading of the Poor-Settlement and Removal bill having, notwithstanding the efforts of the Government, been adjourned to the 28th of April, by a division of 209 to 183. The person to whom the Government is indebted for this defeat, is no other than my Lord Palmerston. 'His lordship,' says *The Times* of this day, 'has *managed* to put himself and his colleagues between two fires (the Tories and the Irish party) without much prospect of leaving them to settle it between themselves.'

We are informed that on the 12th inst. a treaty of triple alliance was signed between France, England and Turkey, but that, notwithstanding the personal application of the Sultan to the Grand Mufti, the latter supported by the *corps* of the Ulemas, refused to issue his *fetva* sanctioning the stipulation about the changes in the situation of the Christians in Turkey, as being in contradiction with the precepts of the Koran. This intelligence must be looked upon as being the more important, as it caused Lord Derby to make the following observation:

I will only express my earnest anxiety that the Government will state whether there is any truth in the report that has been circulated during the last few days that in this convention entered into between England, France and Turkey, there are articles which will be of a nature to establish a protectorate on our part as objectionable at least, as that which, on the part of Russia, we have protested against.

The Times of to-day, while declaring that the policy of the Government is directly opposed to that of Lord Derby, adds: 'We should deeply regret if the bigotry of the Mufti or the Ulemas succeeded in opposing any serious resistance to this policy.'

In order to understand both the nature of the relations between the Turkish Government and the spiritual authorities of Turkey, and the difficulties in which the former is at present involved, with respect to the question of a protectorate over the Christian subjects of the Porte, that question which ostensibly lies at the bottom of all the actual complications in the East, it is necessary to cast a retrospective glance at its past history and development.

The Koran and the Mussulman legislation emanating from it reduce the geography and ethnography of the various people to the simple and convenient distinction of two nations and of two countries; those of the Faithful and of the Infidels. The Infidel is '*harby*,' i.e. the enemy. Islamism proscribes the nation of the Infidels, constituting a state of permanent hostility between the Mussulman and the unbeliever. In that sense the corsair-ships of the Berber States were the holy fleet of Islam. How, then, is the existence of Christian subjects of the Porte to be reconciled with the Koran? 'If a town,' says the Mussulman legislation,

surrenders by capitulation, and its habitants consent to become *rayahs*, that is, subjects of a Mussulman prince without abandoning their creed, they have to pay the *kharatch* (capitation tax), when they obtain a truce with the faithful, and it is not permitted any more to confiscate their estates than to take away their houses . . . In this case their old churches form part of their property, with permission to worship therein. But they are not allowed to erect new ones. They have only authority for repairing them, and to reconstruct their decayed portions. At certain epochs commissaries delegated by the provincial governors are to visit the churches and sanctuaries of the Christians, in order to ascertain that no new buildings have been added under pretext of repairs. If a town is conquered by force, the inhabitants retain their churches, but only as places of abode or refuge, without permission to worship.

Constantinople having surrendered by capitulation, as in like manner has the greater portion of European Turkey, the Christians there enjoy the privilege of living as *rayahs*, under the Turkish Government. This privilege they have exclusively by virtue of their agreeing to accept the Mussulman protection. It is, therefore, owing to this circumstance alone, that the Christians submit to be governed by the Mussulmans according to Mussulman law, that the patriarch of Constantinople, their spiritual chief, is at the same time their political representative and their Chief Justice. Wherever, in the Ottoman Empire, we find an agglomeration of Greek *rayahs*, the Archbishops and Bishops are by law members of the Municipal Councils, and, under the direction of the patriarch, [watch] over the repartition of the taxes imposed upon the Greeks. The patriarch is responsible to the Porte as to the conduct of his co-religionists. Invested with the right of judging the *rayahs* of his Church, he delegates this right to the metropolitans and bishops, in the limits of their dioceses, their sentences being obligatory for the executive officers, kadis, etc., of the Porte to carry out. The punishments which they have the right to pronounce are fines, imprisonment, the bastinade, and exile. Besides, their own church gives them the power of excommunication. Independent of the produce of the fines, they receive variable taxes on the civil and commercial law-suits. Every hierarchic scale among the clergy has its moneyed price. The patriarch pays to the Divan a heavy tribute in order to obtain his investiture, but he sells, in his turn, the archbishoprics and bishoprics to the clergy of his worship. The latter indemnify themselves by the sale of subaltern dignities and the tribute exacted from the popes. These, again, sell by retail the power they have bought from their superiors, and traffic in all acts of their ministry, such as baptisms, marriages, divorces, and testaments.

It is evident from this *exposé* that this fabric of theocracy over the Greek Christians of Turkey, and the whole structure of their society, has its keystone in the subjection of the *rayah* under the Koran, which, in its turn, by treating them as infidels – i.e., as a nation only in a religious sense – sanctioned the combined spiritual and temporal power of their priests. Then, if you abolish their subjection under the Koran by a civil emancipation, you cancel at the same time their subjection to the clergy, and provoke a revolution in their social, political and religious relations, which, in the first instance, must inevitably hand them over to Russia. If you supplant the Koran by a *code civil*, you must occidentalize the entire structure of Byzantine society.

Having described the relations between the Mussulman and his Christian subject, the question arises, what are the relations between the Mussulman and the unbelieving foreigner?

As the Koran treats all foreigners as foes, nobody will dare to present himself in a Mussulman country without having taken his precautions. The first European merchants, therefore, who risked the chances of commerce with such a people, contrived to secure themselves an exceptional treatment and privileges originally personal, but afterward extended to their whole nation. Hence the origin of capitulations. Capitulations are imperial diplomas, letters of privilege, octroyed by the Porte to different European nations, and authorizing their subjects to freely enter Mohammedan countries, and there to pursue in tranquillity their affairs, and to practice their worship. They differ from treaties in this essential point that they are not reciprocal acts contradictorily debated between the contracting parties, and accepted by them on the condition of mutual advantages and concessions. On the contrary, the capitulations are one-sided concessions on the part of the Government granting them, in consequence of which they may be revoked at its pleasure. The Porte has, indeed, at several times nullified the privileges granted to one nation, by extending them to others; or repealed them altogether by refusing to continue their application. This precarious character of the capitulations made them an eternal source of disputes, of complaints on the part of Embassadors, and of a prodigious exchange of contradictory notes and firmans revived at the commencement of every new reign.

It was from these capitulations that arose the right of a *protectorate* of foreign powers, not over the Christian subjects of the Porte – the *rayahs* – but over their co-religionists visiting Turkey or residing there as foreigners. The first power that obtained such a protectorate was France. The capitulations between France and the Ottoman Porte made in 1535, under Soliman the Great and Francis I; in 1604 under Ahmed I and Henry IV; and in 1673 under Mohammed IV and Louis XIV, were renewed, confirmed, recapitulated, and augmented in the compilation of 1740, called 'ancient and recent capitulations and treaties between the Court of France and the Ottoman Porte, renewed and augmented in the year 1740, A.D., and 1153 of the Hegira, translated (the first official translation sanctioned by the Porte) at Constantinople by M. Deval, Secretary Interpreter of the King, and his first Dragoman at the Ottoman Porte.' Art. 32 of this agreement constitutes the right of France to a protectorate over all monasteries professing the Frank religion to whatever nation they may belong, and of the Frank visitors of the Holy Places.

Russia was the first power that, in 1774, inserted the capitulation, imitated after the example of France, into a *treaty* – the treaty of Kainardji. Thus, in 1802, Napoleon thought fit to make the existence and maintenance of the capitulation the subject of an article of treaty, and to give it the character of synallagmatic contract.

In what relation then does the question of the Holy Places stand with the protectorate?

The question of the Holy Shrines is the question of a protectorate over the religious Greek Christian communities settled at Jerusalem, and over the buildings possessed by them on the holy ground, and especially over the Church of the Holy Sepulcher. It is to be understood that possession here does not mean proprietorship, which is denied to the Christians by the Koran, but only the right of *usufruct*. This right of *usufruct* excludes by no means the other communities from worshipping in the same place; the possessors having no other privilege besides that of keeping the *keys*, of repairing and entering the edifices, of kindling the holy lamp, of cleaning the rooms with the broom, and of spreading the carpets, which is an Oriental symbol of possession. In the same manner now, in which Christianity culminates at the Holy Place, the question of the protectorate is there found to have its highest ascension.

Parts of the Holy Places and of the Church of the Holy Sepulcher are possessed by the Latins, the Greeks, the Armenians, the Abyssinians, the Syrians, and the Copts. Between all these diverse pretendents there originated a conflict. The sovereigns of Europe who saw, in this religious quarrel, a question of their respective influences in the Orient, addressed themselves in the first instance to the masters of the soil, to fanatic and greedy Pashas, who abused their position. The Ottoman Porte and its agents adopting a most troublesome *système de bascule* gave judgment in turns favorable to the Latins, Greeks, and Armenians, asking and receiving gold from all hands, and laughing at each of them. Hardly had the Turks granted a firman, acknowledging the right of the Latins to the possession of a contested place, when the Armenians presented themselves with a heavier purse, and instantly obtained a contradictory firman. Same tactics with respect to the Greeks, who knew, besides, as officially recorded in different firmans of the Porte and '*hudjets*' (judgments) of its agents, how to procure false and apocryph titles. On other occasions the decisions of the Sultan's Government were frustrated by the cupidity and ill-will of the Pashas and subaltern agents in Syria. Then it became necessary to resume negotiations, to appoint fresh commissaries, and to make new sacrifices of money. What the Porte formerly did from pecuniary considerations, in our days it has done from fear, with a view to obtain protection and favor. Having done justice to the reclamations of France and the Latins, it hastened to make the same conditions to Russia and the Greeks, thus attempting to escape from a storm which it felt powerless to encounter. There is no sanctuary, no chapel, no stone of the Church of the Holy Sepulcher, that had been left unturned for the purpose of constituting a quarrel between the different Christian communities.

Around the Holy Sepulcher we find an assemblage of all the various sects of Christianity, behind the religious pretensions of whom are concealed as many political and national rivalries.

Jerusalem and the Holy Places are inhabited by nations professing religions: the Latins, the Greeks, Armenians, Copts, Abyssinians, and Syrians. There are 2,000 Greeks, 1,000 Latins, 350 Armenians, 100 Copts, 20 Syrians, and 20 Abyssinians – 3,490. In the Ottoman Empire we find 13,730,000 Greeks, 2,400,000 Armenians, and 900,000 Latins. Each of these is again subdivided. The Greek Church, of which I treated above, the one acknowledging the Patriarch of Constantinople, essentially differs from the Greco-Russian, whose chief spiritual authority is the Czar; and from the Hellens, of whom the King and the Synod of Athens are the chief authorities. Similarly, the Latins are subdivided into the Roman Catholics, United Greeks, and Maronites; and the Armenians into Gregorian and Latin Armenians – the same distinctions holding good with the Copts and Abyssinians. The three prevailing religious nationalities at the Holy Places are the Greeks, the Latins, and the Armenians. The Latin Church may be said to represent principally Latin races, the Greek Church, Slav, Turko-Slav, and Hellenic races; and the other churches, Asiatic and African races.

Imagine all these conflicting peoples beleaguering the

Holy Sepulcher, the battle conducted by the monks, and the ostensible object of their rivalry being a star from the grotto of Bethlehem, a tapestry, a key of a sanctuary, an altar, a shrine, a chair, a cushion – any ridiculous precedence!

In order to understand such a monastical crusade it is indispensable to consider firstly the manner of their living, and secondly, the mode of their habitation. 'All the religious rubbish of the different nations,' says a recent traveler,

live at Jerusalem separated from each other, hostile and jealous, a nomade population, incessantly recruited by pilgrimage or decimated by the plague and oppressions. The European dies or returns to Europe after some years; the pashas and their guards go to Damascus or Constantinople; and the Arabs fly to the desert. Jerusalem is but a place where every one arrives to pitch his tent and where nobody remains. Everybody in the holy city gets his livelihood from his religion – the Greeks or Armenians from the 12,000 or 13,000 pilgrims who yearly visit Jerusalem, and the Latins from the subsidies and alms of their co-religionists of France, Italy, etc.

Besides their monasteries and sanctuaries, the Christian nations possess at Jerusalem small habitations or cells, annexed to the Church of the Holy Sepulcher, and occupied by the monks, who have to watch day and night that holy abode. At certain periods these monks are relieved in their duty by their brethren. These cells have but one door, opening into the interior of the Temple, while the monk guardians receive their food from without, through some wicket. The doors of the Church are closed, and guarded by Turks, who don't open them except for money, and close it according to their caprice or cupidity.

The quarrels between churchmen are the most venomous, said Mazarin. Now fancy these churchmen, who not only have to live upon, but live in, these sanctuaries together!

To finish the picture, be it remembered that the fathers of the Latin Church, almost exclusively composed of Romans, Sardinians, Neapolitans, Spaniards and Austrians, are all of them jealous of the French protectorate, and would like to substitute that of Austria, Sardinia or Naples, the Kings of the two latter countries both assuming the title of King of Jerusalem; and that the sedentary population of Jerusalem numbers about 15,500 souls, of whom 4,000 are Mussulmans and 8,000 Jews. The Mussulmans, forming about a fourth part of the whole, and consisting of Turks, Arabs and Moors, are, of course, the masters in every respect, as they are in no way affected with the weakness of their Government at Constantinople. Nothing equals the misery and the sufferings of the Jews at Jerusalem, inhabiting the most filthy quarter of the town, called *hareth-el-yahoud*, the quarter of dirt, between the Zion and the Moriah, where their synagogues are situated – the constant objects of Mussulman oppression and intolerance, insulted by the Greeks, persecuted by the Latins, and living only upon the scanty alms transmitted by their European brethren. The Jews, however, are not natives, but from different and distant countries, and are only attracted to Jerusalem by the desire of inhabiting the Valley of Jehosaphat, and to die in the very places where the redemptor is to be expected. 'Attending their death,' says a French author, 'they suffer and pray. Their regards turned to that mountain of Moriah, where once rose the temple of Solomon, and which they dare not approach, they shed tears on the misfortunes of Zion, and their dispersion over the world.'

To make these Jews more miserable, England and Prussia appointed, in 1840, an Anglican bishop at Jerusalem, whose avowed object is their conversion. He was dreadfully thrashed in 1845, and sneered at alike by Jews, Christians and Turks. He may, in fact, be stated to have been the first and only cause of a union between all the religions at Jerusalem.

It will now be understood why the common worship of the Christians at the Holy Places resolves itself into a continuance of desperate Irish rows between the diverse sections of the faithful; but that, on the other hand, these sacred rows merely conceal a profane battle, not only of nations but of races; and that the Protectorate of the Holy Places which appears ridiculous to the Occident but all important to the Orientals is one of the phases of the Oriental question incessantly reproduced, constantly stifled, but never solved.

Revolution in Spain

1854

The 'leaders' of the *Assemblée Nationale*, *Times*, and *Journal des Débats* prove that neither the pure Russian party, nor the Russo-Coburg party, nor the Constitutional party are satisfied with the course of the Spanish revolution. From this it would appear that there is some chance for Spain, notwithstanding the contradiction of appearances.

On the 8th [of August] a deputation from the Union Club waited on Espartero to present an address calling for the adoption of universal suffrage. Numerous petitions to the same effect were pouring in. Consequently, a long and animated debate took place at the Council of Ministers. But the partisans of universal suffrage, as well as the partisans of the election law of 1845, have been beaten. The Madrid *Gaceta* publishes a decree for the convocation of the Cortes on the 8th of November preceded by an *exposée* addressed to the Queen. At the elections, the law of 1837 will be followed, with slight modifications. The Cortes are to be one Constituent Assembly, the legislative functions of the Senate being suppressed. Two paragraphs of the law of 1845 have been preserved, viz.: the mode of forming the electoral *mesas* (boards receiving the votes and publishing the returns), and the number of deputies; one deputy to be elected for every 5,000 souls. The Assembly will thus be composed of from 420 to 430 members. According to a circular of Santa Cruz, the Minister of the Interior, the electors must be registered by the 6th of September. After the verification of the lists by the provincial deputations, the electoral lists will be closed on the 12th of September. The elections will take place on the 3d of October, at the chief localities of the Electoral Districts. The scrutiny will be proceeded to on the 16th of October, in the capital of each province. In case of conflicting elections, the new proceedings which will thereby be necessitated, must be terminated by the 30th of October. The *exposé* states expressly that 'the Cortes of 1854, like those of 1837, will save the monarchy; they will be a new bond between the throne and the nation, objects which cannot be questioned or disputed.'

In other words, the Government forbids the discussion of the dynastic question; hence, *The Times* concludes the contrary, supposing that the question will now be between the present dynasty or no dynasty at all – an eventuality which, it is scarcely necessary to remark, infinitely displeases and disappoints the calculations of *The Times*.

The Electoral law of 1837 limits the franchise by the conditions of having a household, the payment of the *mayores cuotas* (the ship taxes levied by the State), and the age of twenty-five years. There are further entitled to a vote: the members of the Spanish Academies of History and of the Artes Nobles, doctors, licentiates in the faculties of Divinity, law, of medicine, members of ecclesiastical chapters, parochial curates and their assistant clergy, magistrates and advocates of two years' standing; officers of the army of a certain standing, whether on service or the retired list; physicians, surgeons, apothecaries of two years' standing; architects, painters and sculptors, honoured with the membership of an academy; professors and masters in any educational establishment, supported by the public funds. Disqualified for the vote by the same law are defaulters to the common pueblo-fund, or to local taxation, bankrupts, persons interdicted by the courts of law for moral or civil incapacity; lastly, all persons under sentence.

It is true that this decree does not proclaim universal suffrage, and that it removes the dynastic question from the forum of the Cortes. Still it is doubtful that even this Assembly will do. If the Spanish Cortes forbore from interfering with the Crown in 1812, it was because the Crown was only nominally represented – the King having been absent for years from Spanish soil. If they forbore in 1837, it was because they had to settle with absolute monarchy before they could think of settling with the constitutional monarchy. With regard to the general situation, *The Times* has truly good reasons to deplore the absence of French centralization in Spain, and that consequently even a victory over revolution in the capital decides nothing with respect to the provinces, so long as that state of 'anarchy' survives there without which no revolution can succeed.

There are, of course, some incidents in the Spanish revolution peculiarly belonging to them. For instance, the combination of robbery with revolutionary transactions – a connection which sprung up in the guerrilla wars against the French invasions, and which was continued by the 'royalists' in 1823, and the Carlists since 1835. No surprise will therefore be felt at the information that great disorders have occurred at Tortosa, in Lower Catalonia. The *Junta Popular* of that city says, in its proclamation of 31st July: 'A band of miserable assassins, availing themselves for pretext of the abolition of the indirect taxes, have seized the town, and trampled upon all laws of society. Plunder, assassination, incendiarism have marked their steps.'

Order, however, was soon restored by the Junta – the citizens arming themselves and coming to the rescue of the feeble garrison of the place. A military commission is sitting, charged with the pursuit and punishment of the authors of the catastrophe of July 30. This circumstance has, of course, given an occasion to the reactionary journals for virtuous declamation. How little they are warranted in this proceeding may be inferred from the remark of the *Messager de Bayonne*, that the Carlists have raised their banner in the provinces of Catalonia, Aragon and Valencia, and precisely in the same contiguous mountains where they had their chief nest in the old Carlist wars. It was the Carlists who gave origin to the *ladrones facciosos*, that combination of robbery and pretended allegiance to an oppressed party in the State. The Spanish guerrillero of all times has had something of the robber since the time of Viriathus; but it is a novelty of Carlist invention that a pure robber should invest himself with the name of guerrillero. The men of the Tortosa affair certainly belong to this class.

At Lerida, Saragossa and Barcelona matters are serious. The two former cities have refused to combine with Barcelona, because the military had the upper hand there. Still it appears that even there Concha is unable to master the storm, and General Dulce is to take his place, the recent popularity of that general being considered as offering more guarantees for a conciliation of the difficulties.

The secret societies have resumed their activity at Madrid, and govern the democratic party just as they did in 1823. The first demand which they have urged the people to make is that all ministers since 1843 shall present their accounts.

The ministry are purchasing back the arms which the people seized on the day of the barricades. In this way they have got possession of 2,500 muskets, formerly in the hands of insurgents. Don Manuel Sagasti, the Ayacucho *Jefe Politico* of Madrid of 1843, has been re-instated in his functions. He has addressed to the inhabitants and the national militia two proclamations, in which he announces his intention of energetically repressing all disorder. The removal of the creatures of Sartorius from the different offices proceeds rapidly. It is, perhaps, the only thing rapidly done in Spain. All parties show themselves equally quick in that line.

Salamanca is not imprisoned, as was asserted. He had been arrested at Aranjuez, but was soon released, and is now at Malaga.

The control of the ministry by popular pressure is proved by the fact, that the Ministers of War, of the Interior, and of Public Works, have effected large displacements and simplifications in their several departments, an event never known in Spanish history before [. . .]

The chief cause of the Spanish revolution was the state of the finances, and particularly the decree of Sartorius, ordering the payment of six months' taxes in advance upon the year. All the public chests were empty when the revolution broke out, notwithstanding the circumstance that no branch of the public service had been paid; nor were the sums destined for any particular service applied to it during the whole of several months. Thus, for instance, the turnpike receipts were never appropriated to the use of keeping up the roads. The moneys set aside for public works shared the same destiny. When the chest of public works was subjected to revision, instead of receipts for executed works, receipts from court favorites were discovered. It is known that financiering has long been the most profitable business in Madrid [. . .]

Spain is the least taxed country of Europe, and the economical question is nowhere so simple as there. The reduction and simplification of the bureaucratic machinery in Spain are the less difficult, as the municipalities traditionally administer their own affairs; so is reform of the tariff, and conscientious application of the *bienes nacionales* not yet alienated. The social question in the modern sense of the word has no foundation in a country with its resources yet undeveloped, and with such a scanty population as Spain – 15,000,000 only [. . .]

Prussia

1856

The strange frenzy which has converted France into a gambling-house, and identified the Napoleonic Empire with the Bourse, has by no means been confined within Gallic boundaries. That plague, unrestrained by political frontiers, has crossed the Pyrenees, the Alps, and the Rhine, and, wonderful to say, has seized upon solid Germany, where speculation in ideas has given way to speculation in stocks, the *summum bonum* to the bonus, the mysterious jargon of dialectics to the no less mysterious jargon of the Exchange, and the aspiration for unity to the passion for dividends. Rhenish Prussia, from its proximity to France, as well as from the high development of its industry and commerce, was the first to catch the disease. Not only did the Cologne bankers enter into a formal alliance with the great swindlers at Paris, by purchasing with them the *Indépendance belge* as their common organ, and establishing an international bank at Luxemburg; not only did they drag into the whirlpool of the Crédit Mobilier all South-Western Germany, but in the limits of Rhenish Prussia and in the Duchy of Westphalia they succeeded so well that at this moment every layer of society, except that formed by the working classes and smaller peasantry, is permeated by the gold mania, so that even the capital of the small middle class, diverted from its customary channels, seeks for wild adventure, and every shopkeeper is turned into an alchemist. That the rest of Prussia has not escaped the contagion will be seen by the following extract from the *Preussische Correspondenz*, a ministerial paper.

Observations recently made on the money market justify the assumption that there is again approaching one of those frightful commercial crises which return periodically. The feverish movement of an immoderate spirit of speculation, first prompted abroad, has, since last year, pervaded Germany to a great extent, and not only the Berlin Bourse and the Prussian capitalists have been dragged into this whirlpool, but also whole classes of society, which, at every former time, endeavored to shun any immediate participation in the hazards of the stock market.

On this apprehension of an imminent financial crisis, the Prussian Government grounded its refusal to allow the establishment of a Crédit Mobilier, the dazzling colors of which were suspected to conceal a swindling purpose. But what is not permitted under one form may be allowed in another; and what is not permitted at Berlin will be tolerated at Leipsic and Hanover. The latest phase of the speculative mania has set in at the close of the war, which, apart from the commercial excitement inseparable from any conclusion of peace – as witnessed in 1802 and 1815 – is this time marked by the peculiar feature that Prussia has formally expressed her wish to throw open her markets to the importation of western capital and speculation. We shall, accordingly, soon hear of the grand Irkutsk trunk-line with branches to Pekin, and other not less monstrous schemes, the question being not what is really designed for execution, but what fresh material may be offered for the spirit of speculation to feed upon. There was nothing wanting but the peace to hurry the great crash apprehended by the Prussian Government.

This uncommon participation by Prussia in the speculative movement of Europe would have been impossible but for the great strides made by its industry of late years. The capital invested in railways alone has been increased from 19,000,000 to 154,000,000 Prussian thalers, in the interval from 1840 to 1854–55. Other railroads at an estimated cost of 54,000,000, are in progress; and the Government have further authorized the construction of new lines at a cost of 57,000,000. Eighty-seven joint-stock companies, with a capital of 83,000,000, have sprung into life since 1849. From 1854–56, nine insurance companies, with a capital of 22,000,000, have been registered. In these last two years, likewise, six joint-stock companies, with a capital of 10,500,000, have commenced to run spinning-mills. From the Cotton Report it will be seen that the quantity of cotton received by the different ports of Europe, has, from 1853–56, varied in the following proportions, according to the return of the first seven months of the year, the export of bales being as follows:

	1853	1854	1855	1856
To England	1,100,000	840,000	963,000	1,131,000
France	255,000	229,000	249,000	354,000
Other European ports	204,000	179,000	167,000	346,000

Hence it follows that the Continent, which in 1853 received only about one third of the cotton exported to England, received in 1856 as much as five eighths of it. To this must be added the cotton reshipped by England to the Continent. The great export to France is only so in appearance, considerable quantities being transported from Havre to Switzerland, Baden, Frankfort and Antwerp. The development of Continental industry as exhibited by the above figures denotes therefore, above all, the increase of German, and chiefly of Prussian industry. The wealth accumulated by the industrial middle classes of late years, is nearly rivaled by the appreciation of land-owners' profits during the war period of dearth and high price. Horses, cattle, live-stock in general, and not least corn, have kept so high in Germany itself, that the influence of foreign markets has hardly been needed to enable the great landholders to roll in gold. It is wealth – the rapid increase of wealth never before experienced by these two classes – which has furnished the basis for the present speculative murrain in Prussia.

The bursting of the bubble will put the Prussian State to a severe test. The different counter-revolutions it has undergone since 1849 have ended in placing the Government in the power of the narrow class of noble landowners, with respect to whom the King, who has done everything to create their supremacy, now finds himself in the same situation as did Louis XVIII toward the *Chambre introuvable*. Frederick William had never the sense to put up with the dry bureaucratic machinery of Government bequeathed him by his father. He has all his life been dreaming of beautifying the Prussian State edifice by some romantico-gothic decoration. The short experience which he has had of his *Herrenhaus*, however, must have satisfied him that in reality the landocracy or *Krautjunkers*, as they are called in Prussia, so far from deeming themselves happy in serving as a mediaeval ornament to the bureaucracy, are striving with all their might to degrade the bureaucracy and make it the simple executor of their class-interests. Hence the split between the Junkers and the Administration; between the King and the Prince of Prussia. To show the Government how much they are in earnest, they have just refused to renew the grant of an additional tax which had been levied during the war – a thing unheard of in constitutional Prussia. They have coolly and deliberately proclaimed the doctrine that they are as much kings over their little estates as the King himself is over the country at large. They insist that the Constitution, while it is to remain a sham for all other classes, must be a reality for themselves. Emancipating themselves from all control of the bureaucracy, they wish to see it weigh with double force on the classes below.

The middle class, who betrayed the revolution of 1848, have now the satisfaction, even while they are accomplishing their social triumph by the unrestrained accumulation of capital, of seeing themselves politically annihilated. Moreover, the *Krautjunkers* delight in every day finding fresh occasions to make them feel their humiliation, even setting aside the common laws of etiquette. When the middle-class spokesmen get up in the House of Deputies, the Junkers leave their benches *en masse*, and when requested at least to listen to opinions contrary to their own, they laugh in the faces of the gentlemen of the Left. When the latter complain of the obstructions put in the way of elections, they are informed that it is simply the duty of the Government to protect the masses from seduction. When they contrast the licentiousness of the aristocratic, with the shackled condition of the liberal press, they are reminded that liberty in a Christian State is not to do as one pleases, but as pleases God and the authorities. One day they are given to understand that 'honor' is the monopoly of an aristocracy; the next day they are stung to the quick by a practical illustration of the exploded theories of a Haller, a de Bonald and a de Maistre. Proud of his philosophical enlightenment, the Prussian citizen has the mortification of seeing the first scientific men driven from the universities, education handed over to a gang of obscurants, ecclesiastical courts meddling with his family concerns, and the police taking him to church on a Sunday. Not content with exempting themselves from taxes so far as they could, the Junkers have packed the middle class in guilds and corporations, adulterated their municipal institutions, abolished the independence and immovability of their Judges, cancelled the religious equality of the different sects, and so forth. If at times their choking anger breaks through their fears, if they occasionally muster enough courage to threaten, from their seats in the Chamber, the Junkers with a coming revolution, they are sneeringly answered that the revolution has as heavy an account to settle with them as with the nobility.

Indeed, the higher middle class is not likely to find itself again, as in 1848, at the head of a Prussian revolution. The peasantry in Eastern Prussia have lost not only all that the revolution of 1848 had brought them in the shape of emancipation, but have been reduced once more, both administratively and judicially, under the direct yoke of the nobility. In Rhenish Prussia, by the attraction of capital toward industrial enterprise, they have sunk deeper into the bondage of the mortgage, at the same rate at which the interest on loans has risen. While in Austria something, at least, has been done to conciliate the peasantry, in Prussia nothing has been left undone to exasperate them. As to the working classes, the Government has prevented them from participating in the profits of their masters by punishing them for strikes, and has systematically excluded them from taking part in political affairs. A disunited dynasty, a Government broken up into hostile camps, the bureaucracy quarreling with the aristocracy, the aristocracy with the middle class – a general commercial crisis, and the disinherited classes brooding in the spirit of rebellion against all the upper layers of society: such is the aspect of Prussia at this hour.

Revolution in Spain [I]

1856

The news brought by the *Asia* yesterday, though later by three days than our previous advices, contains nothing to indicate a speedy conclusion of the civil war in Spain. O'Donnell's coup d'état, although victorious at Madrid, cannot yet be said to have finally succeeded. The French *Moniteur*, which at first put down the insurrection at Barcelona as a mere riot, is now obliged to confess that 'the conflict there was very keen, but that the success of the Queen's troops may be considered as secured.'

According to the version of that official journal the combat at Barcelona lasted from 5 o'clock in the afternoon of July 18 till the same hour on the 21st – exactly three days – when the 'insurgents' are said to have been dislodged from their quarters, and fled into the country, pursued by cavalry. It is, however, averred that the insurgents still hold several towns in Catalonia, including Gerona, Junquera, and some smaller places. It also appears that Murcia, Valencia and Seville have made their *pronunciamientos* [mutinies] against the coup d'état; that a battalion of the garrison of Pampeluna, directed by the Governor of that town on Soria, had pronounced against the Government on the road, and marched to join the insurrection at Saragossa; and lastly that at Saragossa, from the beginning the acknowledged center of resistance, Gen. Falcon had passed in review 16,000 soldiers of the line, reinforced by 15,000 militia and peasants from the environs.

At all events, the French Government considers the 'insurrection' in Spain as not quelled, and Bonaparte, far from contenting himself with the sending of a batch of battalions to line the frontier, has ordered one brigade to advance to the Bidassoa, which brigade is being completed to a division by reinforcements from Montpellier and Toulouse. It seems, also, that a second division has been detached immediately from the army of Lyons, according to orders sent direct from Plombières on the 23d ult., and is now marching toward the Pyrenees, where, by this time, there is assembled a full *corps d'observation* of 25,000 men. Should the resistance to the O'Donnell government be able to hold its ground; should it prove formidable enough to inveigle Bonaparte into an armed invasion of the Peninsula, then the coup d'état of Madrid may have given the signal for the downfall of the coup d'état of Paris.

If we consider the general plot and the *dramatis personae*, this Spanish conspiracy of 1856 appears as the simple revival of the similar attempt of 1843, with some slight alterations of course. Then, as now, Isabella at Madrid and Christina at Paris; Louis Philippe, instead of Louis Bonaparte, directing the movement from the Tuileries; on the one side, Espartero and his *Ayacuchos*; on the other, O'Donnell, Serrano, Concha, with Narvaez then in the proscenium, now in the background. In 1843, Louis Philippe sent two millions of gold by land and Narvaez and his friends by sea, the compact of the

Spanish marriages being settled between himself and Madame Muñoz. The complicity of Bonaparte in the Spanish coup d'état – who has, perhaps, settled the marriage of his cousin Prince Napoleon with a Mdlle. Muñoz, or who at all events, must continue his mission of mimicking his uncle – that complicity is not only indicated by the denunciations hurled by the *Moniteur* for the last two months at the communist conspiracies in Castile and Navarre, by the behavior before, during and after the coup d'état of M. de Turgot, the French Embassador at Madrid, the same man who was the Foreign Minister of Bonaparte during his own coup d'état; by the Duke of Alba, Bonaparte's brother-in-law, turning up as the President of the new *ayuntamiento* at Madrid, immediately after the victory of O'Donnell; by Ros de Olano, an old member of the French party, being the first man offered a place in O'Donnell's Ministry; and by Narvaez being dispatched to Bayonne by Bonaparte as soon as the first news of the affair reached Paris. That complicity was suggested beforehand by the forwarding of large quantities of ammunition from Bordeaux to Bayonne a fortnight in advance of the actual crisis at Madrid. Above all, it is suggested by the plan of operations followed by O'Donnell in his razzia against the people of that city. At the very outset he announced that he would not shrink from blowing up Madrid, and during the fighting he acted up to his word. Now, although a daring fellow, O'Donnell has never ventured upon a bold step without securing a safe retreat. Like his notorious uncle, the hero of treason, he never burnt the bridge when he passed the Rubicon. The organ of combativeness is singularly checked in the O'Donnells by the organs of cautiousness and secretiveness. It is plain that any general who should hold forth the threat of laying the capital in ashes, and fail in his attempt, would forfeit his head. How then did O'Donnell venture upon such delicate ground? The secret is betrayed by the *Journal des Débats*, the special organ of Queen Christina.

O'Donnell expected a great battle, and at the most a victory hotly disputed. Into his provisions there entered the possibility of defeat. If such a misfortune had happened, the Marshal would have abandoned Madrid with the rest of his army, escorting the Queen, and turning toward the northern provinces, with a view to approach the French frontier.

Does not all this look as if he had laid his plan with Bonaparte? Exactly the same plan had been settled between Louis Philippe and Narvaez in 1843, which, again, was copied from the secret convention between Louis XVIII and Ferdinand VII, in 1823.

This plausible parallel between the Spanish conspiracies of 1843 and 1856 once admitted, there are still sufficiently distinct features in the two movements to indicate the immense strides made by the Spanish people within so brief an epoch. These features are: the political character of the last struggle at Madrid; its military importance; and finally, the respective position of Espartero and O'Donnell in 1856 compared with those of Espartero and Narvaez in 1843. In 1843 all parties had become tired of Espartero. To get rid of him a powerful coalition was formed between the *Moderados* and

Progresistas. Revolutionary juntas springing up like mush-rooms in all the towns, paved the way for Narvaez and his retainers. In 1856 we have not only the court and army on the one side against the people on the other, but within the ranks of the people we have the same divisions as in the rest of Western Europe. On the 13th of July the Ministry of Espartero offered its forced resignation; in the night of the 13th and 14th the Cabinet of O'Donnell was constituted; on the morning of the 14th the rumor spread that O'Donnell, charged with the formation of a cabinet, had invited Ryos y Rosas, the ill-omened Minister of the bloody days of July, 1854, to join him. At 11 a.m. the *Gaceta* confirmed the rumor. Then the Cortes assembled, 93 deputies being present. According to the rules of that body, 20 members suffice to call a meeting, and 50 to form a quorum. Besides, the Cortes had not been formally prorogued. Gen. Infante, the President, could not but comply with the universal wish to hold a regular sitting. A proposition was submit-ted to the effect that the new Cabinet did not enjoy the confidence of the Cortes, and that her Majesty should be informed of this resolution. At the same time, the Cortes summoned the National Guard to be ready for action. Their Committee, bearing the resolution of want of confidence, went to the Queen, escorted by a detach-ment of National Militia. While endeavoring to enter the palace they were driven back by the troops of the line, who fired upon them and their escort. This incident gave the signal for the insurrection. The order to com-mence the building of barricades was given at 7 in the evening by the Cortes, whose meeting was dispersed immediately afterward by the troops of O'Donnell. The battle commenced the same night, only one battalion of the National Militia joining the Royal troops. It should be noted that as early as the morning of the 13th, Señor Escosura, the Esparterist Minister of the Interior, had telegraphed to Barcelona and Saragossa that a coup d'état was at hand, and that they must prepare to resist it. At the head of the Madrid insurgents were Señor Madoz and Gen. Valdez, the brother of Escosura. In short, there can be no doubt that the resistance to the coup d'état originated with the Esparterists, the citizens and Liberals in general. While they, with the militia, engaged the line across Madrid from east to west, the workmen under Pucheta occupied the south and part of the north side of the town.

On the morning of the 15th, O'Donnell took the initiative. Even by the partial testimony of the *Débats*, O'Donnell obtained no marked advantage during the first half of the day. Suddenly, at about 1 o'clock, without any perceptible reason, the ranks of the National Militia were broken; at 2 o'clock they were still more thinned, and at 6 o'clock they had completely disappeared from the scene of action, leaving the whole brunt of the battle to be borne by the workmen, who fought it out till 4 in the afternoon of the 16th. Thus there were, in these three days of carnage, two distinct battles – the one of the Liberal Militia of the middle class, supported by the workmen against the army, and the other of the army against the workmen deserted by the militia. As Heine has it: 'It is an old story, but is always new.'

Espartero deserts the Cortes; the Cortes desert the

leaders of the National Guard; the leaders desert their men, and the men desert the people. On the 15th, however, the Cortes assembled again, when Espartero appeared for a moment. He was reminded by Señor Assensio and other members of his reiterated protestations to draw his grand sword of Luchana on the first day when the liberty of the country should be endangered. Espartero called Heaven to witness his unswerving patriotism, and when he left, it was fully expected that he would soon be seen at the head of the insurrection. Instead of this, he went to the house of Gen. Gurrea, where he buried himself in a bomb-proof cellar, à la Palafox, and was heard of no more. The commandants of the militia, who, on the evening before, had employed every means to excite the militiamen to take up arms, now proved as eager to retire to their private houses. At 2½ p.m. Gen. Valdez, who for some hours had usurped the command of the militia, convoked the soldiers under his direct command on the Plaza Mayor, and told them that the man who naturally ought to be at their head would not come forward, and that consequently everybody was at liberty to withdraw. Hereupon the National Guard rushed to their homes and hastened to get rid of their uniforms and hide their arms. Such is the substance of the account furnished by one well-informed authority. Another gives as the reason for this sudden act of submission to the conspiracy, that it was considered that the triumph of the National Guard was likely to entail the ruin of the throne and the absolute preponderance of the Republican Democracy. The *Presse* of Paris also gives us to understand that Marshal Espartero, seeing the turn given to things in the Congress by the Democrats, did not wish to sacrifice the throne, or launch into the hazards of anarchy and civil war, and in consequence did all he could to produce submission to O'Donnell.

It is true that the details as to the time, circumstances, and break-down of the resistance to the coup d'état, are given differently by different writers; but all agree on the one principal point, that Espartero deserted the Cortes, the Cortes the leaders, the leaders the middle class, and that class the people. This furnishes a new illustration of the character of most of the European struggles of 1848–49, and of those hereafter to take place in the Western portion of that continent. On the one hand there are modern industry and trade, the natural chiefs of which, the middle classes, are averse to the military despotism; on the other hand, when they begin the battle against this same despotism, in step the workmen themselves, the product of the modern organization of labor, to claim their due share of the result of victory. Frightened by the consequences of an alliance thus imposed on their unwilling shoulders, the middle classes shrink back again under the protecting batteries of the hated despotism. This is the secret of the standing armies of Europe, which otherwise will be incomprehensible to the future historian. The middle classes of Europe are thus made to understand that they must either surrender to a political power which they detest, and renounce the advantages of modern industry and trade, and the social relations based upon them, or forgo the privileges which the modern organization of the productive powers of society, in its primary phase, has vested in an exclusive class. That this lesson should be taught even from Spain is something equally striking and unexpected.

Revolution in Spain [II]

1856

Saragossa surrendered on August 1, at 1:30 p.m., and thus vanished the last center of resistance to the Spanish counter-revolution. There was, in a military point of view, little chance of success after the defeats at Madrid and Barcelona, the feebleness of the insurrectionary diversion in Andalusia, and the converging advance of overwhelming forces from the Basque provinces, Navarre, Catalonia, Valencia and Castile. Whatever chance there might be was paralyzed by the circumstance that it was Espartero's old aide-de-camp, General Falcon, who directed the forces of resistance; that 'Espartero and Liberty' was given as the battlecry; and that the population of Saragossa had become aware of Espartero's incommensurably ridiculous fiasco at Madrid. Besides, there were direct orders from Espartero's headquarters to his bottle-holders at Saragossa, that they were to put an end to all resistance, as will be seen from the following extract from the *Journal de Madrid* of July 29: 'One of the Esparterist ex-Ministers took part in the negotiations going on between General Dulce and the authorities of Saragossa, and the Esparterist member of the Cortes, Juan Martinez Alonso, accepted the mission of informing the insurgent leaders that the Queen, her

Ministers and her generals, were animated by a most conciliatory spirit.'

The revolutionary movement was pretty generally spread over the whole of Spain. Madrid and La Mancha in Castile; Granada, Seville, Malaga, Cadiz, Jaen, etc., in Andalusia; Murcia and Cartagena in Murcia; Valencia, Alicante, Alzira, etc., in Valencia; Barcelona, Reus, Figueras, Gerona, in Catalonia; Saragossa, Teruel, Huesca, Jaca, etc., in Aragon; Oviedo in Asturias; and Coruña in Galicia. There were no moves in Estremadura, Leon and old Castile, where the revolutionary party had been put down two months ago, under the joint auspices of Espartero and O'Donnell – the Basque provinces and Navarre also remaining quiet. The sympathies of the latter provinces, however, were with the revolutionary cause, although they might not manifest themselves in sight of the French army of observation. This is the more remarkable if it be considered that twenty years ago these very provinces formed the stronghold of Carlism – then backed by the peasantry of Aragon and Catalonia, but who, this time, were most passionately siding with the revolution; and who would have proved a most formidable element of resistance, had not the imbecility of the leaders at Barcelona and Saragossa prevented their energies from being turned to account. Even *The London Morning Herald*, the orthodox champion of Protestantism, which broke lances for the Quixote of the auto-da-fe, Don Carlos, some twenty years ago, has stumbled over that fact, which it is fair enough to acknowledge. This is one of the many symptoms of progress revealed by the last revolution in Spain, a progress the slowness of which will astonish only those not acquainted with the peculiar customs and manners of a country, where 'a la mañana' is the watchword of every day's life, and where everybody is ready to tell you that 'our forefathers needed eight hundred years to drive out the Moors.'

Notwithstanding the general spread of *pronunciamientos*, the revolution in Spain was limited only to Madrid and Barcelona. In the south it was broken by the *cholera morbus*, in the north by the Espartero murrain. From a military point of view, the insurrections at Madrid and Barcelona offer few interesting and scarcely any novel features. On the one side – the army – everything was prepared beforehand; on the other everything was extemporized; the offensive never for a moment changed sides. On the one hand, a well-equipped army, moving easily in the strings of its commanding generals; on the other, leaders reluctantly pushed forward by the impetus of an imperfectly-armed people. At Madrid the revolutionists from the outset committed the mistake of blocking themselves up in the internal parts of the town, on the line connecting the eastern and western extremities – extremities commanded by O'Donnell and Concha, who communicated with each other and the cavalry of Dulce through the external boulevards. Thus the people were cutting off and exposing themselves to the concentric attack preconcerted by O'Donnell and his accomplices. O'Donnell and Concha had only to effect their junction and the revolutionary forces were dispersed into the north and south quarters of the town, and deprived of all further cohesion. It was a distinct feature of the Madrid insurrection that barricades were used sparingly and only at prominent street corners, while the houses were made the centers of resistance; and – what is unheard of in street warfare – bayonet attacks met the assailing columns of the army. But, if the insurgents profited by the experience of the Paris and Dresden insurrections, the soldiers had learned no less by them. The walls of the houses were broken through one by one, and the insurgents were taken in the flank and rear, while the exits into the streets were swept by cannon-shot. Another distinguished feature in this battle of Madrid was that Pucheta, after the junction of Concha and O'Donnell, when he was pushed into the southern (Toledo) quarter of the town, transplanted the guerrilla warfare from the mountains of Spain into the streets of Madrid. The insurrection, dispersed, faced about under some arch of a church, in some narrow lane, on the staircase of a house, and there defended itself to the death.

At Barcelona the fighting was still more intense, there being no leadership at all. Militarily, this insurrection, like all previous risings in Barcelona, perished by the fact of the citadel, Fort Montjuick, remaining in the hands of the army. The violence of the struggle is characterized by the burning of 150 soldiers in their barracks at Gracia, a suburb which the insurgents hotly contested, after being already dislodged from Barcelona. It deserves mention that, while at Madrid [. . .] the proletarians were betrayed and deserted by the bourgeoisie, the weavers of Barcelona declared at the very outset that they would have nothing to do with a movement set on foot by

Esparterists, and insisted on the declaration of the Republic. This being refused, they, with the exception of some who could not resist the smell of powder, remained passive spectators of the battle, which was thus lost – all insurrections at Barcelona being decided by its 20,000 weavers.

The Spanish revolution of 1856 is distinguished from all its predecessors by the loss of all dynastic character. It is known that the movement from 1808 to 1814 was national and dynastic. Although the Cortes in 1812 proclaimed an almost republican Constitution, they did it in the name of Ferdinand VII. The movement of 1820–23, timidly republican, was altogether premature and had against it the masses to whose support it appealed, those masses being bound altogether to the Church and the Crown. So deeply rooted was royalty in Spain, that the struggle between old and modern society, to become serious, needed a testament of Ferdinand VII, and the incarnation of the antagonistic principles in two dynastic branches, the Carlist and Cristina ones. Even to combat for a new principle the Spaniard wanted a time-honored standard. Under these banners the struggle was fought out, from 1833 to 1843. Then there was an end of revolution, and the new dynasty was allowed its trial from 1843 to 1854. In the revolution of July, 1854, there was thus necessarily implied an attack on the new dynasty; but innocent Isabel was covered by the hatred concentrated on her mother, and the people reveled not only in their own emancipation but also in that of Isabel from her mother and the *camarilla*.

In 1856 the cloak had fallen and Isabel herself

confronted the people by the coup d'état that fomented the revolution. She proved the worthy, coolly cruel, and cowardly hypocrite daughter of Ferdinand VII, who was so much given to lying that notwithstanding his bigotry he could never convince himself, even with the aid of the Holy Inquisition, that such exalted personages as Jesus Christ and his Apostles had spoken truth. Even Murat's massacre of the *Madrileños* in 1808 dwindles into an insignificant riot by the side of the butcheries of the 14–16th July, smiled upon by the innocent Isabel. Those days sounded the death-knell of royalty in Spain. There are only the imbecile legitimists of Europe imagining that Isabel having fallen, Don Carlos may rise. They are forever thinking that when the last manifestation of a principle dies away, it is only to give its primitive manifestation another turn.

In 1856, the Spanish revolution has lost not only its dynastic, but also its military character. Why the army played such a prominent part in Spanish revolutions, may be told in a very few words. The old institution of the Captain-Generalships, which made the captains the pashas of their respective provinces; the war of independence against France, which not only made the army the principal instrument of national defense, but also the first revolutionary organization and the center of revolutionary action in Spain; the conspiracies of 1814–19, all emanating from the army; the dynastic war of 1833–40, depending on the armies of both sides; the isolation of the liberal bourgeoisie forcing them to employ the bayonets of the army against clergy and peasantry in the country; the necessity for Cristina and the camarilla to employ bayonets against the Liberals, as the Liberals had employed bayonets against the peasants; the tradition growing out of all these precedents; these were the causes which impressed on revolution in Spain a military, and on the army a pretorian character. Till 1854, revolution always originated with the army, and its different manifestations up to that time offered no external sign of difference beyond the grade in the army whence they originated. Even in 1854 the first impulse still proceeded from the army, but there is the Manzanares manifesto of O'Donnell to attest how slender the base of the military preponderance in the Spanish revolution had become. Under what conditions was O'Donnell finally allowed to stay his scarcely equivocal promenade from Vicálvaro to the Portuguese frontiers, and to bring back the army to Madrid? Only on the promise to immediately reduce it, to replace it by the National Guard, and not to allow the fruits of the revolution, to be shared by the generals. If the revolution of 1854 confined itself thus to the expression of its distrust, only two years later, it finds itself openly and directly attacked by that army – an army that has now worthily entered the lists by the side of the Croats of Radetzky, the Africans of Bonaparte, and the Pomeranians of Wrangel. How far the glories of its new position are appreciated by the Spanish army, is proved by the rebellion of a regiment at Madrid, on the 29th of July, which, not being satisfied with the mere *cigarros* of Isabel, struck for the five franc pieces, and sausages of Bonaparte, and got them, too.

This time, then, the army has been all against the people, or, indeed, it has only fought against them, and the National Guards. In short, there is an end of the revolutionary mission of the Spanish army. The man in whom centered the military, the dynastic, and the bourgeois liberal character of the Spanish revolution – Espartero – has now sunk even lower than the common law of fate would have enabled his most intimate *connoisseurs* to anticipate. If, as is generally rumored, and is very probable, the Esparterists are about to rally under O'Donnell, they will have confirmed their suicide by an official act of their own. They will not save him.

The next European revolution will find Spain matured for cooperation with it. The years 1854 and 1856 were phases of transition she had to pass through to arrive at that maturity.

On Italian Unity

1859

Like the boy and his wolf alarm, the Italians have so repeatedly affirmed that 'Italy is rife with agitation, and on the eve of a revolution,' the crowned heads of Europe have so often prated about a 'settlement of the Italian Question,' that it will not be surprising if the actual appearance of the wolf should be unheeded, and if a real revolution and a general European war should break out and take us unawares! The European aspect of 1859 is decidedly warlike, and, should the hostile bearing, the apparent preparations of France and Piedmont for war with Austria, end in smoke, it is not improbable that the burning hate of the Italians toward their oppressors, combined with their ever-increasing suffering, will find vent in a general revolution. We limit ourselves to a *not improbable* – for, if hope deferred maketh the heart sick, fulfillment of prophecy deferred maketh the mind skeptical. Still, if we are to credit the reports of English, Italian and French journals, the moral condition of Naples is a *facsimile* of her physical structure, and a torrent of revolutionary lava would occasion no more surprise than would a fresh eruption of old Vesuvius. Writers from the Papal States dwell in detail on the increasing abuses of clerical government, and the deep-rooted belief of the Roman population that reform or amelioration is impossible – that a total overthrow of said government is the sole remedy – that this remedy would have been administered long since, but for the presence of Swiss, French and Austrian troops – and that, in spite of these material obstacles, such an attempt may be made at any day or at any hour.

From Venice and Lombardy, the tidings are more definite – and remind us forcibly of the symptoms that marked the close of 1847 and the commencement of 1848 in these provinces. Abstinence from the use of Austrian tobacco and manufactures is universal, also proclamations to the populace to refrain from places of public amusement – studied proofs of hate offered to the Archduke and to all Austrian officials – are carried to such a point that Prince Alfonso Parcia, an Italian nobleman devoted to the House of Hapsburg, dared not, in the public streets, remove his hat as the Archduchess passed, the punishment for which misdemeanor, administered in the form of an order from the Archduke for the Prince's immediate departure from Milan, acts as an incentive to his class to join the popular cry of *fuori i Tedeschi*. ['Out with the Germans'] If we add to these mute demonstrations of popular feeling the daily quarrels between the people and the soldiery, invariably provoked by the former, the revolt of the students of Pavia, and the consequent closing of the Universities, we have before our eyes a reenactment of the prologue to the five days of Milan in 1848.

But while we believe that Italy cannot remain forever in her present condition, since the longest lane must have a turning – while we know that active organization is going on throughout the peninsula, we are not prepared to say whether these manifestations are entirely the spontaneous ebullitions of the popular will, or whether they are stimulated by the agents of Louis Napoleon and of his ally, Count Cavour. Judging from appearances, Piedmont, backed by France, and perhaps by Russia, meditates an attack on Austria in the Spring. From the Emperor's reception of the Austrian Embassador at Paris, it would seem that he harbors no friendly designs toward the Government represented by M. Hübner; from the concentration of so powerful a force at Algiers, it is not unnatural to suppose that hostilities to Austria would commence with an attack on her Italian provinces; the warlike preparations of Piedmont, the all but declarations of war to Austria that emanate daily from the official and semi-official portion of the Piedmontese press, give color to the surmise that the King will avail himself of the first pretext to cross the Ticino. Moreover, the report that Garibaldi, the hero of Montevideo and of Rome, has been summoned to Turin, is confirmed from private and reliable sources. Cavour has had an interview with Garibaldi, informed him of the prospects of a speedy war, and has suggested to him the wisdom of collecting and organizing volunteers. Austria, one of the chief parties concerned, gives evident proof that she lends credence to the rumors. In addition to her 120,000 men, concentrated in her Italian provinces, she is augmenting her forces by every conceivable means; and has just pushed forward a reinforcement of 30,000. The defenses of Venice, Trieste, &c., are being increased and strengthened; and in all her other provinces land-owners and trainers are called on to bring forward their studs, as saddle-horses are required for the cavalry and pioneers. And while, on the one hand, she omits no preparations for resistance in a 'prudent Austrian way,' she is also providing for a possible defeat. From Prussia, the Piedmont of Germany, whose interests are diametrically opposed to her own, she can, at best, hope but for neutrality. The mission of her Embassador, Baron Seebach, to St Petersburg; seems to have failed utterly to win a prospect of success in the case of attack. The schemes of the Czar, in more ways than one, and not the least on the question of the Mediterranean, where he, too, has cast anchor, coincide too nearly with those of his ex-opponent, now fast ally, in Paris, to permit him to defend 'the grateful' Austria. The well-known sympathy of the English *people* with the Italians in their hatred of the *giogo tedesco* ['German yoke'] renders it very doubtful whether any British Ministry would dare to support Austria, anxious as one and all would be to do so. Moreover, Austria, in common with many others, has shrewd suspicions that the would-be 'avenger of Waterloo' has by no means lost sight of his anxiety for the humiliation of 'perfidious Albion' – that, not choosing to beard the lion in his den, he will not shrink from hurling defiance at him in the East, attacking, in conjunction with Russia, the Turkish Empire (despite his oaths to maintain that empire inviolate), thus bringing half the British forces into action on the Eastern battlefield, while from Cherbourg he keeps the other half in forced inaction, guarding the British coasts. Therefore, in the case of actual war, Austria has the uncomfortable feeling that she must rely on herself alone; and one of her many expedients for suffering the least possible loss, in case of defeat, is worthy of notice for its impudent sagacity. The barracks, palaces, arsenals and other official buildings throughout Venetian Lombardy, the erection and maintenance of which have taxed the Italians exorbitantly, are, nevertheless, considered the property of the Empire. At this moment the Government is compelling the different municipalities to purchase all these buildings at a fabulous price, alleging as its motive that it intends to *rent* instead of owning them for the future. Whether the municipalities will ever see a farthing of the *rent*, even if Austria retains her sway, is doubtful at best; but, should she be driven from all, or from any part of her Italian territory, she will congratulate herself on her cunning scheme for converting a large portion of her forfeited treasure into portable cash. It is asserted, moreover, that she is using her utmost efforts to inspire the Pope, the King of Naples, the Dukes of Tuscany, Parma and Modena, with her own resolution to resist to the uttermost all attempts on the part of the people or the crowned heads to change the existing order of things in Italy. But none knows better than Austria herself how bad would be the best efforts of these poor tools to make head against the tide of popular insurrection or foreign interference. And, while war on Austria is the fervent aspiration of every true Italian heart, we cannot doubt that a large majority of Italians look upon the prospects of a war, begun by France and Piedmont, as doubtful, to say the least, in its results. While none conscientiously believe that the murderer of Rome can by any human process be transformed into the Savior of Lombardy, a small faction favor Louis Napoleon's designs of placing Murat on the throne of Naples, profess to believe in his intention to remove the Pope from Italy or to confine him to the City and Campagna of Rome, and of assisting Piedmont to add the whole of Northern Italy to her dominions. Then there is a party, small but honest, who imagine that the idea of an Italian crown dazzles Victor Emmanuel, as it was supposed to dazzle his father; who believe that he anxiously awaits the first opportunity to unsheathe his sword for its attainment, and that it is with this sole end in view that the King will avail himself of help from France, or any other help, to achieve this coveted treasure. A much larger class, numbering adherents throughout the oppressed provinces of Italy, especially in Lombardy and among the Lombard emigration, having no particular faith in the Piedmontese King or Piedmontese monarchy, yet say: 'Be their aims what they may, Piedmont has an army of 100,000 men, a navy, arsenals, and treasure; let her throw down the gauntlet to Austria; we will follow her to the battlefield: if she is faithful, she shall have her reward; if she falls short of her mission, the nation will be strong enough to continue the battle once begun and follow it up to victory.'

The Italian National party, on the contrary, denounce as a national calamity the inauguration of an Italian War of Independence under the auspices of France and Piedmont. The point at issue with them is not, as is often erroneously supposed, whether Italy, once free from the foreigners, shall be united under a republican or monarchical form of government, but that the means proposed must fail to win Italy for the Italians, and can at best only exchange one foreign yoke for another equally oppressive. They believe that the man of the 2d of December will never make war at all, unless compelled by the growing impatience of his army, or by the threatening aspect of the French people; that, thus compelled, his choice of Italy as the theater of war would have for its object the fulfillment of his uncle's scheme – the making of the Mediterranean a 'French lake' – which end would be accomplished by seating Murat on the throne of Naples; that, in dictating terms to Austria, he seeks the completion of his revenge, commenced in the Crimea, for the treaties of 1815, when Austria was one of the parties who dictated to France terms humiliating in the extreme for the Bonaparte family. They look upon Piedmont as the mere cat's-paw of France – convinced that, his own ends achieved, not daring to assist Italy to attain that liberty which he denies to France, Napoleon III will conclude a peace with Austria and stifle all efforts of the Italians to carry on the war. If Austria shall have at all maintained her ground, Piedmont must content herself with the addition of the Duchies of Parma and Modena to her present territory; but, should Austria be worsted in the fight, that peace will be concluded on the Adige, which will leave the whole of Venice and part of Lombardy in the hands of the hated Austrians. This *peace upon the Adige*, they affirm, is already tacitly agreed on between Piedmont and France. Confident as this party feels of the triumph of the nation in the event of a national war against Austria, they maintain that, should that war be commenced with Napoleon for Inspirer, and the King of Sardinia for Dictator, the Italians will have put it out of their own power to move a step in opposition to their accepted heads, to impede in any manner the wiles of diplomacy, the capitulations, treaties and the reriveting of their chains which must result therefrom; and they point to the conduct of Piedmont toward Venice and Milan in 1848, and at Novara in 1849, and urge their countrymen to profit by that bitter experience of their fatal trust in princes. All their efforts are directed to complete the organization of the peninsula, to induce the people to unite in one supreme effort, and not to commence the struggle until they feel themselves capable of initiating the great national insurrection which, while deposing the Pope, Bomba & Co., would render the armies, navies and war material of the respective provinces available for the extermination of the foreign foe. Regarding the Piedmontese army and people as ardent champions of Italian liberty, they feel that the King of Piedmont will thus have ample scope for aiding the freedom and independence of Italy, if he chooses; should he prove reactionary, they know that the army and people will side with the nation. Should he justify the faith reposed in him by his partisans, the Italians will not be backward in testifying their gratitude in a tangible form. In any case, the nation will be in a situation to decide on its own destinies, and feeling, as they do, that a successful revolution in Italy will be the signal for a general struggle on the part of all the oppressed nationalities to rid themselves of their oppressors, they have no fear of interference on the part of France, since Napoleon III will have too much home business on his hands to meddle with the affairs of other nations, even for the furtherance of his own ambitious aims. *A chi tocca-tocca?* ['Who is to begin?'] as the Italians say. We will not venture to predict whether the revolutionists or the regular armies will appear first on the field. What seems pretty certain is, that a war begun in any part of Europe will not end where it commences; and if, indeed, that war is inevitable, our sincere and heartfelt desire is, that it may bring about a true and just settlement of the Italian question and of various other questions, which, until settled, will continue from time to time to disturb the peace of Europe, and consequently impede the progress and prosperity of the whole civilized world.

The North American Civil War

1861

For months the leading weekly and daily papers of the London press have been reiterating the same litany on the American Civil War. While they insult the free states of the North, they anxiously defend themselves against the suspicion of sympathizing with the slave states of the South. In fact, they continually write two articles: one article, in which they attack the North, and another article, in which they excuse their attacks on the North. *Qui s'excuse s'accuse.*

In essence the extenuating arguments read: The war between the North and South is a tariff war. The war is, further, not for any principle, does not touch the question of slavery, and in fact turns on Northern lust for sovereignty. Finally, even if justice is on the side of the North, does it not remain a vain endeavor to want to subjugate eight million Anglo-Saxons by force! Would not separation of the South release the North from all connection with Negro slavery and ensure for it, with its twenty million inhabitants and its vast territory, a higher, hitherto scarcely dreamt-of, development? Accordingly, must not the North welcome secession as a happy event, instead of wanting to overrule it by a bloody and futile civil war?

Point by point we will probe the plea of the English press.

The war between North and South – so runs the first excuse – is a mere tariff war, a war between a protectionist system and a free trade system, and Britain naturally stands on the side of free trade. Shall the slave-owner enjoy the fruits of slave labor in their entirety or shall he be cheated of a portion of these by the protectionists of the North? That is the question which is at issue in this war. It was reserved for *The Times* to make this brilliant discovery. *The Economist*, *The Examiner*, *The Saturday Review*, and *tutti quanti* ['all such'] expounded the theme further. It is characteristic of this discovery that it was made, not in Charleston, but in London. Naturally, in America everyone knew that from 1846 to 1861 a free trade system prevailed, and that Representative Morrill carried his protectionist tariff through Congress only in 1861, after the rebellion had already broken out. Secession, therefore, did not take place because the Morrill tariff had gone through Congress, but, at most, the Morrill tariff went through Congress because secession had taken place. When South Carolina had its first attack of secession in 1831, the protectionist tariff of 1828 served it, to be sure, as a pretext, but only as a pretext, as is known from a statement of General Jackson. This time, however, the old pretext has in fact not been repeated. In the Secession Congress at Montgomery all reference to the tariff question was avoided, because the cultivation of sugar in Louisiana, one of the most influential Southern states, depends entirely on protection.

But, the London press pleads further, the war of the United States is nothing but a war for the forcible maintenance of the Union. The Yankees cannot make up their minds to strike fifteen stars from their standard. They want to cut a colossal figure on the world stage. Yes, it would be different if the war was waged for the abolition of slavery! The question of slavery, however, as *The Saturday Review* categorically declares among other things, has absolutely nothing to do with this war.

It is above all to be remembered that the war did not originate with the North, but with the South. The North finds itself on the defensive. For months it had quietly looked on while the secessionists appropriated the Union's forts, arsenals, shipyards, customs houses, pay offices, ships, and supplies of arms, insulted its flag and took prisoner bodies of its troops. Finally the secessionists resolved to force the Union government out of its passive attitude by a blatant act of war, and *solely for this reason* proceeded to the bombardment of Fort Sumter near Charleston. On April 11 (1861) their General Beauregard had learnt in a meeting with Major Anderson, the commander of Fort Sumter, that the fort was only supplied with provisions for three days more and accordingly must be peacefully surrendered after this period. In order to forestall this peaceful surrender, the secessionists opened the bombardment early on the following morning (April 12), which brought about the fall of the fort in a few hours. News of this had hardly been telegraphed to Montgomery, the seat of the Secession Congress, when War Minister Walker publicly declared in the name of the new Confederacy: 'No man can say where *the war opened today* will end.' At the same time he prophesied 'that before the first of May the flag of the Southern Confederacy will wave from the dome of the

old Capitol in Washington and within a short time perhaps also from the Faneuil Hall in Boston.' Only now
ensued the proclamation in which Lincoln called for
75,000 men to defend the Union. The bombardment of
Fort Sumter cut off the only possible constitutional way
out, namely the convocation of a general convention of
the American people, as Lincoln had proposed in his
inaugural address. For Lincoln there now remained only
the choice of fleeing from Washington, evacuating Maryland and Delaware and surrendering Kentucky, Missouri,
and Virginia, or of answering war with war.

The question of the principle of the American Civil
War is answered by the battle slogan with which the
South broke the peace. Stephens, the Vice-President
of the Southern Confederacy, declared in the Secession
Congress that what essentially distinguished the Constitution newly hatched at Montgomery from the
Constitution of the Washingtons and Jeffersons was that
now for the first time slavery was recognized as an
institution good in itself, and as the foundation of the
whole state edifice, whereas the revolutionary fathers,
men steeped in the prejudices of the eighteenth century,
had treated slavery as an evil imported from England
and to be eliminated in the course of time. Another
matador of the South, Mr Spratt, cried out: 'For us it is
a question of founding a great slave republic.' If, therefore, it was indeed only in defense of the Union that
the North drew the sword, had not the South already
declared that the continuance of slavery was no longer
compatible with the continuance of the Union?

Just as the bombardment of Fort Sumter gave the

signal for the opening of the war, the election victory of the *Republican* Party of the North, the election of Lincoln as President, gave the signal for secession. On November 6, 1860, Lincoln was elected. On November 8, 1860, a message telegraphed from South Carolina said: 'Secession is regarded here as a settled thing;' on November 10 the legislature of Georgia occupied itself with secession plans, and on November 13 a special session of the legislature of Mississippi was convened to consider secession. But Lincoln's election was itself only the result of a split in the *Democratic* camp. During the election struggle the Democrats of the North concentrated their votes on *Douglas*, the Democrats of the South concentrated their votes on *Breckinridge*, and to this splitting of the Democratic votes the Republican Party owed its victory. Whence came, on the one hand, the preponderance of the *Republican* Party in the North? Whence, on the other, the disunion *within* the *Democratic* Party, whose members, North and South, had operated in conjunction for more than half a century?

Under the presidency of Buchanan the sway that the South had gradually usurped over the Union through its alliance with the Northern Democrats attained its zenith. The last Continental Congress of 1787 and the first Constitutional Congress of 1789–90 had legally excluded slavery from all Territories of the republic northwest of the Ohio. (Territories, as is known, is the name given to the colonies lying within the United States itself which have not yet attained the level of population constitutionally prescribed for the formation of autonomous states.) The so-called Missouri Compromise (1820), in consequence of which Missouri became one of the States of the Union as a slave state, excluded slavery from every remaining Territory north of 36°30' latitude and west of the Missouri. By this compromise the area of slavery was advanced several degrees of longitude, while, on the other hand, a geographical boundary-line to its future spread seemed quite definitely drawn. This geographical barrier, in its turn, was thrown down in 1854 by the so-called Kansas–Nebraska Bill, the initiator of which was St[ephen] A. Douglas, then leader of the Northern Democrats. The Bill, which passed both Houses of Congress, repealed the Missouri Compromise, placed slavery and freedom on the same footing, commanded the Union government to treat them both with equal indifference, and left to the sovereignty of the people, that is, the majority of the settlers, to decide whether or not slavery was to be introduced in a Territory. Thus, for the first time in the history of the United States, every geographical and legal limit to the extension of slavery in the Territories was removed. Under this new legislation the hitherto free Territory of New Mexico, a Territory five times as large as the State of New York, was transformed into a slave Territory, and the area of slavery was extended from the border of the Mexican Republic to 38° north latitude. In 1859 New Mexico received a slave code that vies with the statute-books of Texas and Alabama in barbarity. Nevertheless, as the census of 1860 proves, among some 100,000 inhabitants New Mexico does not count even half a hundred slaves. It had therefore sufficed for the South to send some adventurers with a few slavers over the border, and then with the help of the central government in Washington and of its officials and contractors in New Mexico to drum together a sham popular representation to impose slavery and with it the rule of the slaveholders on the Territory.

However, this convenient method did not prove applicable in other Territories. The South accordingly went a step further and appealed from Congress to the Supreme Court of the United States. This Court, which numbers nine judges, five of whom belong to the South, had long been the most willing tool of the slaveholders. It decided in 1857, in the notorious Dred Scott case, that every American citizen possesses the right to take with him into any Territory any property recognized by the Constitution. The Constitution, it maintained, recognizes slaves as property and obliges the Union government to protect this property. Consequently, on the basis of the Constitution, slaves could be forced to labor in the Territories by their owners, and so every individual slaveholder was entitled to introduce slavery into hitherto free Territories against the will of the majority of the settlers. The right to exclude slavery was taken from the Territorial legislatures and the duty to protect pioneers of the slave system was imposed on Congress and the Union government.

If the Missouri Compromise of 1820 had extended the geographical boundary-line of slavery in the Territories, if the Kansas–Nebraska Bill of 1854 had erased every geographical boundary-line and set up a political barrier instead, the will of the majority of the settlers, now the Supreme Court of the United States, by its decision of

1857, tore down even this political barrier and transformed all the Territories of the republic, present and future, from nurseries of free states into nurseries of slavery.

At the same time, under, Buchanan's government the severer law on the surrendering of fugitive slaves enacted in 1850 was ruthlessly carried out in the states of the North. To play the part of slave-catchers for the Southern slaveholders appeared to be the constitutional calling of the North. On the other hand, in order to hinder as far as possible the colonization of the Territories by free settlers, the slaveholders' party frustrated all the so-called free-soil measures, i.e., measures which were to secure for the settlers a definite amount of uncultivated state land free of charge.

In the foreign, as in the domestic, policy of the United States, the interests of the slaveholders served as the guiding star: Buchanan had in fact obtained the office of President through the issue of the Ostend Manifesto, in which the acquisition of Cuba, whether by purchase or by force of arms, was proclaimed as the great task of national policy. Under his government northern Mexico was already divided among American land speculators, who impatiently awaited the signal to fall on Chihuahua, Coahuila, and Sonora. The unceasing piratical expeditions of the filibusters against the states of Central America were directed no less from the White House at Washington. In the closest connection with this foreign policy, whose manifest purpose was conquest of new territory for the spread of slavery and of the slaveholders' rule, stood the *reopening of the slave trade*, secretly supported by the Union government. St[ephen] A. Douglas himself declared in the American Senate on August 20, 1859: 'During the last year more Negroes have been imported from Africa than ever before in any single year, even at the time when the slave trade was still legal. The number of slaves imported in the last year totalled fifteen thousand.'

Armed spreading of slavery abroad was the avowed aim of national policy; the Union had in fact become the slave of the 300,000 slaveholders who held sway over the South. A series of compromises, which the South owed to its alliance with the Northern Democrats, had led to this result. On this alliance all the attempts, periodically repeated since 1817, to resist the ever increasing encroachments of the slaveholders had hitherto come to grief. At length there came a turning point.

For hardly had the Kansas–Nebraska Bill gone through, which wiped out the geographical boundary-line of slavery and made its introduction into new Territories subject to the will of the majority of the settlers, when armed emissaries of the slaveholders, border rabble from Missouri and Arkansas, with bowie-knife in one hand and revolver in the other, fell upon Kansas and sought by the most unheard-of atrocities to dislodge its settlers from the Territory colonized by them. These raids were supported by the central government in Washington. Hence a tremendous reaction. Throughout the North, but particularly in the Northwest, a relief organization was formed to support Kansas with men, arms, and money. Out of this relief organization arose the *Republican Party*, which therefore owes its origin to the struggle for Kansas. After the attempt to transform Kansas into a *slave Territory* by force of arms had failed, the South sought to achieve the same result by political intrigues. Buchanan's government, in particular, exerted its utmost efforts to have Kansas included in the States of the Union as a *slave state* with a slave constitution imposed on it. Hence renewed struggle, this time mainly conducted in Congress at Washington. Even St[ephen] A. Douglas, the chief of the Northern Democrats, now (1857–58) entered the lists against the government and his allies of the South, because imposition of a slave constitution could have been contrary to the principle of sovereignty of the settlers passed in the Nebraska Bill of 1854. Douglas, Senator for Illinois, a Northwestern state, would naturally have lost all his influence if he had wanted to concede to the South the right to steal by force of arms or through acts of Congress Territories colonized by the North. As the struggle for Kansas, therefore, called the *Republican Party* into being, it at the same time occasioned the first *split within the Democratic Party* itself.

The Republican Party put forward its first platform for the presidential election in 1856. Although its candidate, John Frémont, was not victorious, the huge number of votes cast for him at any rate proved the rapid growth of the Party, particularly in the Northwest. At their second National Convention for the presidential elections (May 17, 1860), the Republicans again put forward their platform of 1856, only enriched by some additions. Its principal contents were the following: Not a foot of fresh territory is further conceded to slavery.

The filibustering policy abroad must cease. The re-opening of the slave trade is stigmatized. Finally, free-soil laws are to be enacted for the furtherance of free colonization.

The vitally important point in this platform was that not a foot of fresh terrain was conceded to slavery; rather it was to remain once and for all confined within the boundaries of the states where it already legally existed. Slavery was thus to be formally interned; but continual expansion of territory and continual spread of slavery beyond its old limits is a law of life for the slave states of the Union.

The cultivation of the southern export articles, cotton, tobacco, sugar, etc., carried on by slaves, is only remunerative as long as it is conducted with large gangs of slaves, on a mass scale and on wide expanses of a naturally fertile soil, which requires only simple labor. Intensive cultivation, which depends less on fertility of the soil than on investment of capital, intelligence, and energy of labor, is contrary to the nature of slavery. Hence the rapid transformation of states like Maryland and Virginia, which formerly employed slaves in the production of export articles, into states which raise slaves to export them into the deep South. Even in South Carolina, where the slaves form four-sevenths of the population, the cultivation of cotton has been almost completely stationary for years due to the exhaustion of the soil. Indeed, by force of circumstances South Carolina has already been transformed in part into a slave-raising state, since it already sells slaves to the sum of four million dollars yearly to the states of the extreme South and Southwest.

As soon as this point is reached, the acquisition of new Territories becomes necessary, so that one section of the slaveholders with their slaves may occupy new fertile lands and that a new market for slave-raising, therefore for the sale of slaves, may be created for the remaining section. It is, for example, indubitable that without the acquisition of Louisiana, Missouri, and Arkansas by the United States, slavery in Virginia and Maryland would have become extinct long ago. In the Secessionist Congress at Montgomery, Senator Toombs, one of the spokesmen of the South, strikingly formulated the economic law that commands the constant expansion of the territory of slavery. 'In fifteen years,' said he, 'without a great increase in slave territory, either the slaves must be permitted to flee from the whites, or the whites must flee from the slaves.'

As is known, the representation of the individual states in the Congress House of Representatives depends on the size of their respective populations. As the populations of the free states grow far more quickly than those of the slave states, the number of Northern Representatives was bound to outstrip that of the Southern very rapidly. The real seat of the political power of the South is accordingly transferred more and more to the American Senate, where every state, whether its population is great or small, is represented by two Senators. In order to assert its influence in the Senate and, through the Senate, its hegemony over the United States, the South therefore required a continual formation of new slave states. This, however, was only possible through conquest of foreign lands, as in the case of Texas, or through the transformation of the Territories belonging to the United States first into slave Territories and later into slave states, as in the case of Missouri, Arkansas, etc. *John Calhoun*, whom the slaveholders admire as their stateman *par excellence*, stated as early as February 19, 1847, in the Senate, that the Senate alone placed a balance of power in the hands of the South, that extension of the slave territory was necessary to preserve this equilibrium between South and North in the Senate, and that the attempts of the South at the creation of new slave states by force were accordingly justified.

Finally, the number of actual slaveholders in the South of the Union does not amount to more than 300,000, a narrow oligarchy that is confronted with many millions of so-called poor whites, whose numbers have been constantly growing through concentration of landed property and whose condition is only to be compared with that of the Roman plebeians in the period of Rome's extreme decline. Only by acquisition and the prospect of acquisition of new Territories, as well as by filibustering expeditions, is it possible to square the interests of these 'poor whites' with those of the slaveholders, to give their restless thirst for action a harmless direction and to tame them with the prospect of one day becoming slaveholders themselves.

A strict confinement of slavery within its old terrain, therefore, was bound according to economic law to lead to its gradual extinction, in the political sphere to annihilate the hegemony that the slave states exercised through the Senate, and finally to expose the slaveholding oligarchy within its own states to threatening perils

from the 'poor whites.' In accordance with the principle
that any further extension of slave Territories was to be
prohibited by law, the Republicans therefore attacked
the rule of the slaveholders at its root. The Republican
election victory was accordingly bound to lead to open
struggle between North and South. And this election
victory, as already mentioned, was itself conditioned by
the split in the Democratic camp.

The Kansas struggle had already caused a split between the slaveholders' party and the Democrats of the
North allied to it. With the presidential election of 1860,
the same strife now broke out again in a more general
form. The Democrats of the North, with Douglas as
their candidate, made the introduction of slavery into
Territories dependent on the will of the majority of the
settlers. The slaveholders' party, with Breckinridge as
their candidate, maintained that the Constitution of the
United States, as the Supreme Court had also declared,
brought slavery legally in its train; in and of itself slavery
was already legal in all Territories and required no special
naturalization. While, therefore, the Republicans prohibited any extension of slave Territories, the Southern
party laid claim to all Territories of the republic as legally
warranted domains. What they had attempted by way
of example with regard to Kansas, to force slavery on a
Territory through the central government against the
will of the settlers themselves, they now set up as law
for all the Territories of the Union. Such a concession
lay beyond the power of the *Democratic* leaders and
would only have occasioned the desertion of their army
to the Republican camp. On the other hand, Douglas's

'settlers' sovereignty' could not satisfy the slaveholders' party. What it wanted to effect had to be effected within the next four years under the new President, could only be effected by the resources of the central government, and brooked no further delay. It did not escape the slaveholders that a new power had arisen, the *Northwest*, whose population, having almost doubled between 1850 and 1860, was already pretty well equal to the white population of the slave states – a power that was not inclined either by tradition, temperament, or mode of life to let itself be dragged from compromise to compromise in the manner of the old Northeastern states. The Union was still of value to the South only so far as it handed over Federal power to it as a means of carrying out the slave policy. If not, then it was better to make the break now than to look on at the development of the Republican Party and the upsurge of the Northwest for another four years and begin the struggle under more unfavorable conditions. The slaveholders' party therefore played *va banque*! ['betting it all'] When the Democrats of the North declined to go on playing the part of the 'poor whites' of the South, the South secured Lincoln's victory by splitting the vote, and then took this victory as a pretext for drawing the sword from the scabbard.

The whole movement was and is based, as one sees, on the *slave question*. Not in the sense of whether the slaves within the existing slave states should be emancipated outright or not, but whether the 20 million free men of the North should submit any longer to an oligarchy of 300,000 slaveholders; whether the vast Territories of the republic should be nurseries for free states or for slavery; finally, whether the national policy of the Union should take armed spreading of slavery in Mexico, Central and South America as its device [. . .]

The News and Its Effect in London

1861

Since the declaration of war against Russia I never witnessed an excitement throughout all the strata of English society equal to that produced by the news of the *Trent* affair,* conveyed to Southampton by the *La Plata* on the 27th inst. At about 2 o'clock p.m., by means of the electric telegraph, the announcement of the 'untoward event' was posted in the news-rooms of all the British Exchanges. All commercial securities went down, while the price of saltpeter went up. Consols declined ¾ per cent, while at Lloyds war risks of five guineas were demanded on vessels from New York. Late in the evening the wildest rumors circulated in London, to the effect that the American Minister had forthwith been sent his passports, that orders had been issued for the immediate seizure of all American ships in the ports of the United Kingdom, and so forth. The cotton friends of Secession at Liverpool improved the opportunity for holding, at ten minutes' notice, in the cotton salesroom of the Stock Exchange, an indignation meeting, under the presidency of Mr Spence, the author of some obscure

---

* The USS *Jacinto* illegally boarded the British mail ship *Trent* and two confederate diplomats en route to Britain were abducted. For a time war between the USA and UK appeared possible.

pamphlet in the interest of the Southern Confederacy. Commodore Williams, the Admiralty Agent on board the *Trent*, who had arrived with the *La Plata*, was at once summoned to London.

On the following day, the 28th of November, the London press exhibited, on the whole, a tone of moderation strangely contrasting with the tremendous political and mercantile excitement of the previous evening. The Palmerston papers, *Times*, *Morning Post*, *Daily Telegraph*, *Morning Advertiser*, and *Sun*, had received orders to calm down rather than to exasperate. *The Daily News*, by its strictures on the conduct of the *San Jacinto*, evidently aimed less at hitting the Federal Government than clearing itself of the suspicion of 'Yankee prejudices,' while *The Morning Star*, John Bright's organ, without passing any judgment on the policy and wisdom of the 'act,' pleaded its lawfulness. There were only two exceptions to the general tenor of the London press. The Tory-scribblers of *The Morning Herald* and *The Standard*, forming in fact one paper under different names, gave full vent to their savage satisfaction of having at last caught the 'republicans' in a trap, and finding a *casus belli*, ready cut out. They were supported by but one other journal, *The Morning Chronicle*, which for years had tried to prolong its checkered existence by alternately selling itself to the poisoner Palmer and the Tuileries. The excitement on the Exchange greatly subsided in consequence of the pacific tone of the leading London papers. On the same 28th of Nov., Commander Williams attended at the Admiralty, and reported the circumstances of the occurrence in the old Bahama Channel. His report, together with the written depositions of the officers on board the *Trent*, were at once submitted to the law officers of the Crown, whose opinion, late in the evening, was officially brought under the notice of Lord Palmerston, Earl Russell and other members of the Government.

On the 29th of November there was to be remarked some slight change in the tone of the ministerial press. It became known that the law officers of the Crown, on a technical ground, had declared the proceedings of the frigate *San Jacinto illegal*, and that later in the day, the Cabinet, summoned to a general council, had decided to send by next steamer to Lord Lyons instructions to conform to the opinion of the English law officers. Hence the excitement in the principal places of business, such as the Stock Exchange, Lloyd's, the Jerusalem, the Baltic, etc., set in with redoubled force, and was further stimulated by the news that the projected shipments to America of saltpeter had been stopped on the previous day, and that on the 29th a general order was received at the Custom-House prohibiting the exportation of this article to any country except under certain stringent conditions. The English funds further fell ¾, and at one time a real panic prevailed in all the stock markets, it having become impossible to transact any business in some securities, while in all descriptions a severe depression of prices occurred. In the afternoon a recovery in the stock market was due to several rumours, but principally to the report that Mr Adams had expressed his opinion that the act of the *San Jacinto* would be disavowed by the Washington Cabinet.

On the 30th of November (to-day) all the London

papers, with the single exception of *The Morning Star*, put the alternative of reparation by the Washington Cabinet or – *war*.

Having summed up the history of the events from the arrival of the *La Plata* to the present day; I shall now proceed to recording opinions. There were, of course, two points to be considered – on the one hand the law, on the other hand the policy, of the seizure of the Southern Commissioners on board an English mail steamer.

As to the legal aspect of the affair, the first difficulty mooted by the Tory press and *The Morning Chronicle* was that the United States had never recognized the Southern Secessionists as belligerents, and, consequently, could not claim belligerent rights in regard to them.

This quibble was at once disposed of by the Ministerial press itself. 'We,' said *The Times*, 'have already recognized these Confederate States as a belligerent power, and we shall, when the time comes, recognize their Government. Therefore we have imposed on ourselves all the duties and inconveniences of a power neutral between two belligerents.'

Hence, whether or not the United States recognize the Confederates as belligerents, they have the right to insist upon England submitting to all the duties and inconveniences of a neutral in maritime warfare.

Consequently, with the exceptions mentioned, the whole London press acknowledge the right of the *San Jacinto* to overhaul, visit, and search the *Trent*, in order to ascertain whether she carried goods or persons belonging to the category of 'contraband of war.' *The Times*'s insinuation that the English law of decisions 'was given *under circumstances very different from* those which now occur;' that 'steamers did not then exist,' and mail vessels, 'carrying letters wherein all the nations of the world have immediate interest, were unknown;' that 'we (the English) were *fighting for existence*, and did in those days *what we should not* allow others to do,' was not seriously thrown out. Palmerston's private *Moniteur*, *The Morning Post*, declared on the same day that mail steamers were simple merchantmen, not sharing the exemption from the right of search of men-of-war and transports. The *right of search*, on the part of the *San Jacinto*, was in point of fact, conceded by the London press as well as the law officers of the Crown. The objection that the *Trent*, instead of sailing from a belligerent to a belligerent port, was, on the contrary, bound from a neutral to a neutral port, fell to the ground by Lord Stowell's decision that the right of search is intended to ascertain the destination of a ship.

In the second instance, the question arose whether by firing a round shot across the bows of the *Trent*, and subsequently throwing a shell, bursting close to her, the *San Jacinto* had not violated the usages and courtesies appurtenant to the exercise of the right of visitation and search. It was generally conceded by the London press that, since the details of the event have till now been only ascertained by the depositions of one of the parties concerned, no such minor question could influence the decision to be arrived at by the British Government.

The right of search, exercised by the *San Jacinto*, thus being conceded, what had she to look for? For *contraband of war*, presumed to be conveyed by the *Trent*. What is contraband of war? Are the *dispatches* of a belligerent Government contraband of war? Are the *persons* carrying those dispatches contraband of war? And, both questions being answered in the affirmative, do those dispatches and the bearers of them continue to be contraband of war, if found on a merchant ship bound from a neutral port to a neutral port? The London press admits that the decisions of the highest legal authorities on both sides of the Atlantic are so contradictory, and may be claimed with such appearance of justice for both the affirmative and the negative, that, at all events, a *prima facie* case is made out for the *San Jacinto*.

Concurrently with this prevalent opinion of the English press, the English Crown lawyers have altogether dropped the material question, and only taken up the formal question. They assert that the law of nations was not violated in *substance*, but in *form* only. They have arrived at the conclusion that the *San Jacinto* failed in seizing, on her own responsibility, the Southern Commissioners, instead of taking the *Trent* to a Federal port and submitting the question to a Federal Prize-Court, no armed cruiser having a right to make himself a Judge at sea. A violation in the *procedure* of the *San Jacinto* is, therefore, all that is imputed to her by the English Crown lawyers, who, in my opinion, are right in their conclusion. It might be easy to unearth precedents, showing England to have similarly trespassed on the formalities of maritime law; but violations of law can never be allowed to supplant the law itself.

The question may now be mooted, whether the

reparation demanded by the English Government – that is, the restitution of the Southern Commissioners – be warranted by an injury which the English themselves avow to be of *form* rather than of *substance*? A lawyer of the Temple, in to-day's *Times*, remarks, in respect to this point:

If the case is not so clearly in our favor as that a decision in the American Court condemning the vessel would have been liable to be questioned by us as manifestly contrary to the laws of nations, then the irregularity of the American Captain in allowing the *Trent* to proceed to Southampton, clearly redounded to the advantage of the British owners and the British passengers. Could we in such a case find a ground of international quarrel in an error of procedure which in effect told in our own favor?

Still, if the American Government must concede, as it seems to me, that Capt. Wilkes has committed a violation of maritime law, whether formal or material, their fair fame and their interest ought alike to prevent them from nibbling at the terms of the satisfaction to be given to the injured party. They ought to remember that they do the work of the Secessionists in embroiling the United States in a war with England, that such a war would be a godsend to Louis Bonaparte in his present difficulties, and would, consequently, be supported by all the official weight of France; and, lastly, that, what with the actual force under the command of the British on the North American and West Indian stations, what with the forces of the Mexican Expedition, the English Government would have at its disposal an overwhelming maritime power.

As to the policy of the seizure in the Bahama Channel, the voice not only of the English but of the European press is unanimous in expressions of bewilderment at the strange conduct of the American Government, provoking such tremendous international dangers, for gaining the bodies of Messrs Mason, Slidell & Co., while Messrs Yancey and Mann are strutting in London. *The Times* is certainly right in saying: 'Even Mr Seward himself must know that the voices of these Southern Commissioners, sounding from their captivity, are a thousand times more eloquent in London and in Paris than they would have been if they had been heard at St James's and the Tuileries.'

The people of the United States having magnanimously submitted to a curtailment of their own liberties in order to save their country, will certainly be no less ready to turn the tide of popular opinion in England by openly avowing, and carefully making up for, an international blunder the vindication of which might realize the boldest hopes of the rebels.

Progress of Feeling in England

1861

The friends of the United States on this side of the Atlantic anxiously hope that conciliatory steps will be taken by the Federal Government. They do so not from a concurrence in the frantic crowing of the British press over a war incident, which, according to the English Crown lawyers themselves, resolves itself into a mere error of procedure, and may be summed up in the words that there has been a breach of international law, because Capt. Wilkes, instead of taking the *Trent*, her cargo, her passengers, and the Commissioners, did only take the Commissioners. Nor springs the anxiety of the well-wishers of the Great Republic from an apprehension lest, in the long run, it should not prove able to cope with England, although backed by the civil war; and, least of all, do they expect the United States to abdicate, even for a moment, and in a dark hour of trial, the proud position held by them in the council of nations. The motives that prompt them are of quite a different nature.

In the first instance, the business next in hand for the United States is to crush the rebellion and to restore the Union. The wish uppermost in the minds of the Slaveocracy and their Northern tools was always to plunge the United States into a war with England. The first step of England as soon as hostilities broke out would be to recognize the Southern Confederacy, and the second to terminate the blockade. Secondly, no general, if not forced, will accept battle at the time and under the conditions chosen by his enemy. 'A war with America,' says *The Economist*, a paper deeply in Palmerston's confidence, 'must always be one of the most lamentable incidents in the history of England; but if it is to happen, *the present is certainly the period at which it will do us the minimum of harm, and the only moment in our joint annals at which it would confer on us an incidental and partial compensation.*'

The very reasons accounting for the eagerness of England to seize upon any decent pretext for war at this 'only moment' ought to withhold the United States from forwarding such a pretext at this 'only moment.' You go not to war with the aim to do your enemy '*the minimum of harm,*' and, even to confer upon him by the war, '*an incidental and partial compensation.*' The opportunity of the moment would all be on one side, on the side of your foe. Is there any great strain of reasoning wanted to prove that an internal war raging in a State is the least opportune time for entering upon a foreign war? At every other moment the mercantile classes of Great Britain would have looked upon a war against the United States with the utmost horror. Now, on the contrary, a large and influential party of the mercantile community has for months been urging on the Government to violently break the blockade, and thus provide the main branch of British industry with its raw material. The fear of a curtailment of the English export trade to the United

States has lost its sting by the curtailment of that trade having already actually occurred. 'They' (the Northern States), says *The Economist*, 'are wretched customers, instead of good ones.' The vast credit usually given by English commerce to the United States, principally by the acceptance of bills drawn from China and India, has been already reduced to scarcely a fifth of what it was in 1857. Last, not least, Decembrist France, bankrupt, paralyzed at home, beset with difficulty abroad, pounces upon an Anglo-American war as a real godsend, and, in order to buy English support in Europe, will strain all her power to support 'Perfidious Albion' on the other side of the Atlantic. Read only the French newspapers. The pitch of indignation to which they have wrought themselves in their tender care for the 'honor of England,' their fierce diatribes as to the necessity on the part of England to revenge the outrage on the Union Jack, their vile denunciations of everything American, would be truly appalling, if they were not ridiculous and disgusting at the same time. Lastly, if the United States give way in this instance, they will not derogate one iota of their dignity. England has reduced her complaint to a mere *error of procedure, a technical blunder* of which she has made herself systematically guilty in all her maritime wars, but against which the United States have never ceased to protest, and which President Madison, in his message inaugurating the war of 1812, expatiated upon as one of the most shocking breaches of international law. If the United States may be defended in paying England with her own coin, will they be accused for magnanimously disavowing, on the part of a single

American captain, acting on his own responsibility, what they always denounced as a systematic usurpation on the part of the British Navy! In point of fact, the gain of such a procedure would be all on the American side. England, on the one hand, would have acknowledged the right of the United States to capture and bring to adjudication before an American prize court every English ship employed in the service of the Confederation. On the other hand, she would, once for all, before the eyes of the whole world, have practically resigned a claim which she was not brought to desist from either in the peace of Ghent, in 1814, or the transactions carried on between Lord Ashburton and Secretary Webster in 1842. The question then comes to this: Do you prefer to turn the 'untoward event' to your own account, or, blinded by the passions of the moment, turn it to the account of your foes at home and abroad?

Since this day week [. . .] British consols have again lowered, the decline, compared with last Friday, amounting to 2 per cent, the present prices being 89¾ to ⅞ for money and 90 to 90⅛ for the new account on the 9th of January. This quotation corresponds to the quotation of the British consols during the first two years of the Anglo-Russian war. This decline is altogether due to the warlike interpretation put upon the American papers conveyed by the last mail, to the exacerbating tone of the London press, whose moderation of two days' standing was but a feint, ordered by Palmerston, to the dispatch of troops for Canada, to the proclamation forbidding the export of arms and materials for gunpowder and lastly, to the daily ostentatious statements concerning the formidable preparations for war in the docks and maritime arsenals.

Of one thing you may be sure, Palmerston wants a legal pretext for a war with the United States, but meets in the Cabinet councils with a most determinate opposition on the part of Messrs Gladstone and Milner Gibson, and, to a less degree, of Sir Cornwall Lewis. 'The noble viscount' is backed by Russell, an abject tool in his hands, and the whole Whig Coterie. If the Washington Cabinet should furnish the desired pretext, the present Cabinet will be sprung, to be supplanted by a Tory Administration. The preliminary steps for such a change of scenery have been already settled between Palmerston and Disraeli. Hence the furious war-cry of *The Morning Herald* and *The Standard*, those hungry wolves howling at the prospect of the long-missed crumbs from the public almoner.

Palmerston's designs may be shown up by calling into memory a few facts. It was he who insisted upon the proclamation, acknowledging the Secessionists as belligerents, on the morning of the 14th of May, after he had been informed by telegraph from Liverpool that Mr Adams would arrive at London on the night of the 13th May. He, after a severe struggle with his colleagues, dispatched 3,000 men to Canada, an army ridiculous, if intended to cover a frontier of 1,500 miles, but a clever sleight-of-hand if the rebellion was to be cheered, and the Union to be irritated. He, many weeks ago, urged Bonaparte to propose a joint armed intervention 'in the internecine struggle,' supported that project in the Cabinet council, and failed only in carrying it by the resistance of his colleagues. He and Bonaparte then resorted to the Mexican intervention as a *pis aller*. That operation served two purposes, by provoking just resentment on the part of the Americans, and by simultaneously furnishing a pretext for the dispatch of a squadron, ready, as *The Morning Post* has it, 'to perform whatever duty the hostile conduct of the Government of Washington may require us to perform in the waters of the Northern Atlantic.' At the time when that expedition was started, *The Morning Post*, together with *The Times* and the smaller fry of Palmerston's press slaves, said that it was a very fine thing, and a philanthropic thing into the bargain, because it would expose the slaveholding Confederation to two fires – the Anti-Slavery North and the Anti-Slavery force of England and France. And what says the very same *Morning Post*, this curious compound of Jenkins and Rhodomonte, of plush and swash, in its to-day's issue, on occasion of Jefferson Davis's address? Hearken to the Palmerston oracle:

We must look to this intervention as one that may be in operation during a considerable period of time; and while the Northern Government is too distant to admit of its attitude entering materially into this question, the Southern Confederation, on the other hand, stretches for a great distance along the frontier of Mexico, so as to render its friendly disposition to the authors of the insurrection of no slight consequence. The Northern Government has invariably railed at our neutrality, but the Southern with statesmanship and moderation has recognized in it all that we could do for either party; and whether with a view to our transactions in Mexico, or to our relations with the Cabinet at Washington, the *friendly forbearance* of the Southern Confederacy is an important point in our favor.

I may remark that the *Nord* of December 3 – a Russian paper, and consequently a paper initiated into Palmerston's designs – insinuates that the Mexican expedition was from the first set on foot, not for its ostensible purpose, but for a war against the United States.

Gen. Scott's letter had produced such a beneficent reaction in public opinion, and even on the London Stock Exchange, that the conspirators of Downing street and the Tuileries found it necessary to let loose the *Patrie*, stating with all the airs of knowledge derived from official sources that the seizure of the Southern Commissioners from the *Trent* was directly authorized by the Washington Cabinet.

English Public Opinion

1862

The news of the pacific solution of the *Trent* conflict was, by the bulk of the English people, saluted with an exultation proving unmistakably the unpopularity of the apprehended war and the dread of its consequences. It ought never to be forgotten in the United States that at least the *working classes* of England, from the commencement to the termination of the difficulty, have never forsaken them. To them it was due that, despite the poisonous stimulants daily administered by a venal and reckless press, not one single public war meeting could be held in the United Kingdom during all the period that peace trembled in the balance. The only war meeting convened on the arrival of the *La Plata*, in the cotton salesroom of the Liverpool Stock Exchange, was a corner meeting where the cotton jobbers had it all to themselves. Even at Manchester, the temper of the working classes was so well understood that an insulated attempt at the convocation of a war meeting was almost as soon abandoned as thought of.

Wherever public meetings took place in England, Scotland, or Ireland, they protested against the rabid war-cries of the press, against the sinister designs of the Government, and declared for a pacific settlement of the pending question. In this regard, the two last meetings held, the one at Paddington, London, the other at New-castle-upon-Tyne, are characteristic. The former meeting applauded Mr Washington Wilkes's argumentation that England was not warranted in finding fault with the seizure of the Southern Commissioners; while the Newcastle meeting almost unanimously carried the resolution – firstly, that the Americans had only made themselves guilty of a *lawful* exercise of the right of search and seizure; secondly, that the captain of the *Trent* ought to be punished for his violation of English neutrality, as proclaimed by the Queen. In ordinary circumstances, the conduct of the British workingmen might have been anticipated from the natural sympathy the popular classes all over the world ought to feel for the only popular Government in the world.

Under the present circumstances, however, when a great portion of the British working classes directly and severely suffers under the consequences of the Southern blockade; when another part is indirectly smitten by the curtailment of the American commerce, owing, as they are told, to the selfish 'protective policy' of the Republicans; when the only remaining democratic weekly, *Reynolds's* paper, has sold itself to Messrs Yancey and Mann, and week after week exhausts its horse-powers of foul language in appeals to the working classes to urge the Government, for their own interests, to war with the Union – under such circumstances, simple justice requires to pay a tribute to the sound attitude of the British working classes, the more so when contrasted with the hypocritical, bullying, cowardly, and stupid conduct of the official and well-to-do John Bull.

What a difference in this attitude of the people from what it had assumed at the time of the Russian complication! Then *The Times*, *The Post*, and the other Yellow-plushes of the London press, whined for peace, to be rebuked by tremendous war meetings all over the country. Now they have howled for war, to be answered by peace meetings denouncing the liberticide schemes and the Pro-Slavery sympathy of the Government. The grimaces cut by the augurs of public opinion at the news of the pacific solution of the *Trent* case are really amusing.

In the first place, they must needs congratulate themselves upon the dignity, common sense, good will, and moderation, daily displayed by them for the whole interval of a month. They *were* moderate for the first two days after the arrival of the *La Plata*, when Palmerston felt uneasy whether any legal pretext for a quarrel was to be picked. But hardly had the crown lawyers hit upon a legal quibble, when they opened a charivari unheard of since the anti-Jacobin war. The dispatches of the English Government left Queenstown in the beginning of December. No official answer from Washington could possibly be looked for before the commencement of January. The new incidents arising in the interval told all in favor of the Americans. The tone of the Transatlantic Press, although the Nashville affair might have roused its passions, was calm. All facts ascertained concurred to show that Capt. Wilkes had acted on his own hook. The position of the Washington Government was delicate. If it resisted the English demands, it would complicate the civil war by a foreign war. If it gave way, it might damage its popularity at home, and appear to cede to pressure from abroad. And the Government thus placed, carried, at the same time, a war which must enlist the warmest sympathies of every man, not a confessed ruffian, on its side.

Common prudence, conventional decency, ought, therefore, to have dictated to the London press, at least for the time separating the English demand from the American reply, to anxiously abstain from every word calculated to heat passion, breed ill-will, complicate the difficulty. But no! That 'inexpressibly mean and groveling' press, as William Cobbett, and he was a *connoisseur*, calls it, really boasted of having, when in fear of the compact power of the United States, humbly submitted to the accumulated slights and insults of Pro-Slavery Administrations for almost half a century, while now, with the savage exultation of cowards, they panted for taking their revenge on the Republican Administration, distracted by a civil war. The record of mankind chronicles no self-avowed infamy like this.

One of the yellow-plushes, Palmerston's private *Moniteur – The Morning Post –* finds itself arraigned on a most ugly charge from the American papers. John Bull has never been informed – on information carefully withheld from him by the oligarchs that lord it over him – that Mr Seward, without awaiting Russell's dispatch, had disavowed any participation of the Washington Cabinet in the act of Capt. Wilkes. Mr Seward's dispatch arrived at London on December 19. On the 20th December, the rumor of this 'secret' spread on the Stock Exchange. On the 21st, the yellow-plush of *The Morning Post* stepped forward to gravely herald that 'the dispatch in question does not in any way whatever refer to the outrage on our mail packet.'

In *The Daily News*, *The Morning Star*, and other London journals, you will find yellow-plush pretty sharply handled, but you will not learn from them what people out of doors say. They say that *The Morning Post* and *The Times*, like the *Patrie* and the *Pays*, duped the public not only to politically mislead them, but to fleece them in the monetary line on the Stock Exchange, in the interest of their patrons.

The brazen *Times*, fully aware that during the whole crisis it had compromised nobody but itself, and given another proof of the hollowness of its pretensions of influencing the real people of England, plays to-day a trick which here, at London, only works upon the laughing muscles, but on the other side of the Atlantic, might be misinterpreted. The 'popular classes' of London, the 'mob', as the yellow-plush call them, have given unmistakable signs – have even hinted in newspapers – that they should consider it an exceedingly seasonable joke to treat Mason (by the by, a distant relative of Palmerston, since the original Mason had married a daughter of Sir W. Temple), Slidell & Co. with the same demonstrations Haynau received on his visit at Barclay's brewery. *The Times* stands aghast at the mere idea of such a shocking incident, and how does it try to parry it? It admonishes the people of England not to overwhelm Mason, Slidell & Co. with any sort of public *ovation*! *The Times* knows that its to-day's article will form the laughing-stock of all the tap-rooms of London. But never mind! People on the other side of the Atlantic may, perhaps, fancy that the magnanimity of *The Times* has saved them from the affront of public ovations to Mason, Slidell & Co., while, in point of fact, *The Times* only intends saving those gentlemen from public insult!

So long as the *Trent* affair was undecided, *The Times*, *The Post*, *The Herald*, *The Economist*, *The Saturday Review*, in fact the whole of the fashionable, hireling press of London, had tried its utmost to persuade John Bull that the Washington Government, even if it willed, would prove unable to keep the peace, because the Yankee mob would not allow it, and because the Federal Government was a mob Government. Facts have now given them the lie direct. Do they now atone for their malignant slanders against the American people? Do they at least confess the errors which yellow-plush, in presuming to judge of the acts of a free people, could not but commit? By no means. They now unanimously discover that the American Government, in not anticipating England's demands, and not surrendering the Southern traitors as soon as they were caught, missed a great occasion, and deprived its present concession of all merit. Indeed, yellow plush! Mr Seward disavowed the act of Wilkes before the arrival of the English demands, and at once declared himself willing to enter upon a conciliatory course; and what did you do on similar occasions? When, on the pretext of impressing English sailors on board American ships – a pretext not at all connected with maritime belligerent rights, but a downright, monstrous usurpation against all international law – the *Leopard* fired its broadside at the *Chesapeake*, killed six, wounded twenty-one of her sailors, and seized the pretended Englishmen on board the *Chesapeake*, what did the English Government do? That outrage was perpetrated on the 20th of June, 1807. The real satisfaction, the surrender of the sailors, &c., was only offered on November 8, 1812, five years later. The British Government, it is true, disavowed at once the act of Admiral Berkeley, as Mr Seward did in regard to Capt. Wilkes; but, to punish the Admiral, it removed him from an inferior to a superior rank. England, in proclaiming her Orders in Council, distinctly confessed that they were outrages on the rights of neutrals in general, and of the United States in particular; that they were forced upon her as measures of retaliation against Napoleon, and that she would feel but too glad to revoke them whenever Napoleon should revoke his encroachments on neutral rights. Napoleon did revoke them, as far as the United States were concerned, in the Spring of 1810. England persisted in her avowed outrage on the maritime rights of America. Her resistance lasted from 1806 to 23d of June, 1812 – after, on the 18th of June, 1812, the United States had declared war against England. England abstained, consequently, in this case for six years, not from atoning for a confessed outrage, but from discontinuing it. And this people talk of the magnificent occasion missed by the American Government! Whether in the wrong or in the right, it was a cowardly act on the part of the British Government to back a complaint grounded on pretended technical blunder, and a mere error of procedure, by an ultimatum, by a demand for the surrender of the prisoners. The American Government might have reasons to accede to that demand; it could have none to anticipate it.

By the present settlement of the *Trent* collision, the question underlying the whole dispute, and likely to again occur – the belligerent rights of a maritime power against neutrals – has not been settled. I shall, with your permission, try to survey the whole question in a subsequent letter. For the present, allow me to add that, in my opinion, Messrs Mason and Slidell have done great service to the Federal Government. There was an influential war party in England, which, what for commercial, what for political reasons, showed eager for a fray with the United States. The *Trent* affair put that party to the test. It has failed. The war passion has been discounted on a minor issue, the steam has been let off, the vociferous fury of the oligarchy has raised the suspicions of English democracy, the large British inter-ests connected with the United States have made a stand, the true character of the civil war has been brought home to the working classes, and last, not least, the dangerous period when Palmerston rules single-headed without being checked by Parliament, is rapidly drawing to an end. That was the only time in which an English war for the slaveocrats might have been hazarded. It is now out of question.